Ultimate HEAVY METAL Guitars

THE GUITARISTS WHO ROCKED THE WORLD

Pete Prown

CONTENTS

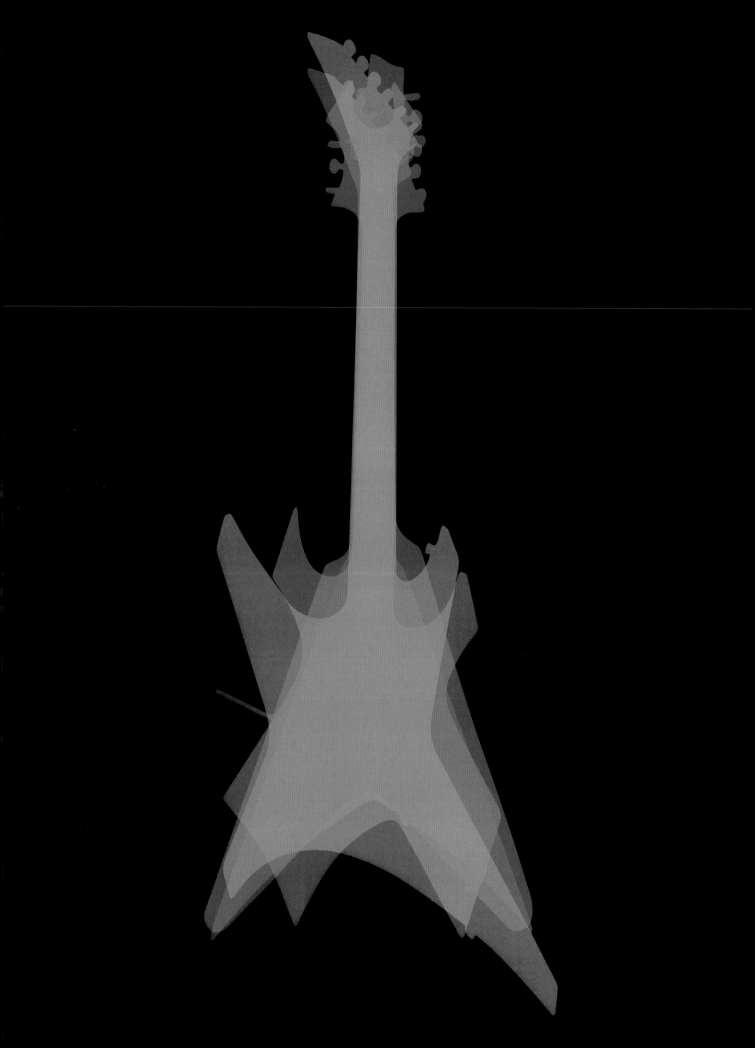

LOUD & PROUD

Born in the hellfire of 1960s rebellion, heavy metal became the perfect storm of loud, distorted electric guitars; jackhammer drums; and gut-punching bass. Crowned with the caterwaul of a screaming frontman (or woman!), metal has become a global sound, commanding millions of fans—often in direct opposition to rock critics, who routinely bashed the genre in its formative years. The more the critics hated it, the more its fans came to revere this style of guitar-intensive, take-no-prisoners rock and roll.

The caricature of metal as a chaotic, barbaric noise is, of course, nonsense. It is a vital, complex form of music that emerged out of psychedelic rock and the blues revival. In the hands of master musicians, it can be loud and brutal or soft and introspective, something perfected by one of it's genre-carving bands, Led Zeppelin, renowned as much for their acoustic songs as high-voltage anthems. Even blunt-force-trauma acts like Black Sabbath, Deep Purple, and Metallica played riffs that were both heavy and melodic. Witness Sabbath's "Laguna Sunrise" or Metallica's "One."

This brings us to the book you're holding in your mitts, *Ultimate Heavy Metal Guitars*. Here we'll detail over a half-century of metal and hard-rock wizards, how the music has evolved, and most importantly, the incredible guitars played. To avoid argument, this book won't judge who *is* and who *isn't* a metal guitarist or band—especially since the musical term *heavy metal* actually *predates* Led Zeppelin and Black Sabbath by several years. For our purposes, if their rock and roll is cranked and brain crushing, they're in the club, be it acid rock like Iron Butterfly and Steppenwolf, the prog of Rush and Kansas, or grunge by Alice in Chains. Naturally the axes of Jimmy Page, Tony Iommi, Eddie Van Halen, James Hetfield, and Slash will be thoroughly unpacked and put under the metal microscope. In these pages, *loud is loud*.

Welcome to the jungle, folks. ⚡

THE DAWN OF HEAV

The quintessential symbol of metal is the solidbody electric guitar, an instrument comprising a body and neck of "tonewood," so named for the musical properties of the wood itself. That block is then carved (by a guitar builder known as a *luthier*) into myriad shapes and fitted with strings, hardware, and magnetic pickups capable of sounds ranging from fat and smooth to trebly and piercing. Finally, the solidbody is often finished in bodacious colors and graphics. Plugged into another iconic piece of gear—an amplifier head and pair of enormous 4 x 12 speaker cabinets, configured into a 100-watt stack—the electric guitar and ensuing sonic blast took metal from simply a loud style of music into something of beauty and sophistication. A universe of portable and affordable effects pedals—our much-loved "stompboxes"—only sweetens the deal.

The solidbody guitar is more than a mere symbol of the music—it's a critical tool to get the job done. Throughout the '60s, the balance of power between guitar types began to shift away from the quieter timbres of hollow- and semi-hollowbody construction toward the easily mass-produced solidbody. It's an instrument that not only withstood high volumes but elegantly *shaped* this punishing sound into real music.

By 1970, high-volume heroes like Jimi Hendrix, Jeff Beck, Pete Townshend, and Eric Clapton had already proven they could fill arenas with decibels, and *without* uncontrolled feedback, by pairing those amp stacks to a solidbody—notably, the venerable Fender Stratocaster, Gibson Les Paul, and Gibson SG. To this day, these three models remain the cornerstones of metal-guitar design, be it a modern super-strat or countless Flying V and Explorer clones. Most modern solidbody designs are derived from the Gibson archetype (humbucking pickups, mahogany body, and built-in neck) or the Fender archetype (single-coil pickups, ash or alder body, and bolt-on maple neck).

With this musical technology in place, the thunder of metal was looming on the horizon. The gear, bands, and guitar heroes were finally coalescing. A storm of hurricane force was about to smash into rock and roll, and, better yet, there was nothing the critics could do about it. ⚡

ERIC CLAPTON

Over a long and extraordinary career, Eric Clapton has gone to great lengths to explain he had nothing to do with the coming of heavy metal . . . *except*, of course, he had so much to do with it. While Clapton's only actual heavy band was Cream—a trio that melded blues, psychedelia, extended improvisation, and British Invasion pop—his fiery, blues-based approach became scripture for future hard rock players. There's a reason why so many guitarists name-check Clapton as a critical influence.

A historic moment transpired in the spring of 1966, when John Mayall's Bluesbreakers entered Decca Studios in London with the ex-Yardbirds guitarist, barely out of his teens. Clapton brought a simple rig: a 1960 Les Paul 'burst, a Marshall 45-watt combo (Model 1962), and possibly a Dallas Rangemaster treble booster. Critically Clapton de-

By the fall of 1966, "Slowhand" was a member of the first super-group, Cream, along with bassist Jack Bruce and drummer Ginger Baker, releasing their debut, *Fresh Cream*. This album codified that Les Paul/Marshall combination, heard on "Spoonful," giving the solidbody guitar a sonic girth never achieved before. The guitarist's trademark "woman tone"—a warm sound created by rolling back the bridge pickup's Tone knob—only made the statement more compelling. By next summer's *Disraeli Gears*, Clapton got his hands on a newfangled Vox wah pedal for "Tales of Brave Ulysses," ratcheting up the bar yet again.

Cream's apex was 1968's *Wheels of Fire*, a double LP that cemented the rudiments of heavy guitar for all perpetuity. It's all here: the PAF humbuckers of Clapton's painted 1964 Les Paul/SG, known as "The Fool"

vember, he was playing a red Gibson ES-335, another iconic axe. By 1970 he had become a dyed-in-the-wool Stratocaster player (inspired by his hero Buddy Guy) and has been playing Fenders ever since.

For amps, Marshalls have been a part of the picture from John Mayall's Bluesbreakers onward. Returning to high-voltage FM rock in the 1980s and 1990s—after a decade exploring mellow reggae, blues, the Tulsa sound, and ballads (usually with Fender or Music Man amps)—Clapton reliably has a full Marshall 100-watt stack onstage behind him, mixed with Fender tweed combos. This back-line fuels his Fender Eric Clapton Signature Stratocaster, which has a built-in 25 dB mid-boost circuit to deliver fatter, more Gibson-like tones when warranted. Despite topping the pop charts with lighter material, the shadow of Cream still lingers in his live and studio rigs.

CLAPTON'S CRUNCHY TONE CONTRIBUTED TO THE RISE OF METAL AS MUCH AS ANYONE.

manded that his amp was recorded at a stunningly loud volume, heard on tracks like "All Your Love" and "Key to Love." Clapton's bold blues phrases, bends, and vibrato—combined with this huge-sounding rig—created the watershed moment when heavy guitar tone was born. There had been dirty fuzz and overdriven sounds before, but this is when that cranked-to-11, overdriven-tube goodness was caught on tape for the first time. Truly a historic moment in guitar.

(the '60 sunburst had been stolen); Marshall JTM45/100 and Super Lead heads and 4 x 12 cabinets; and a wah-wah pedal, all pumping out big chords, pentatonic lightning, and just-about-perfect wrist vibrato. Clapton's solos in "White Room" and "Cross-roads" remain incontestable proof of his six-string innovations.

Putting the SG down, Clapton bought a Gibson Firebird at a Philadelphia tour stop in April 1968, and by Cream's farewell concert that No-

In retrospect Clapton's crunchy tone emerged from the primordial ooze of psychedelia and, combined with soul-searing blues bends and power chords, contributed to the rise of metal as much as anyone else, despite his protests to the contrary. Every guitarist who overdrives a tube amp and bends a string owes a debt to that cheeky English lad who first cranked a Marshall back in '66. ⚡

ERIC CLAPTON WITH CREAM, 1967.

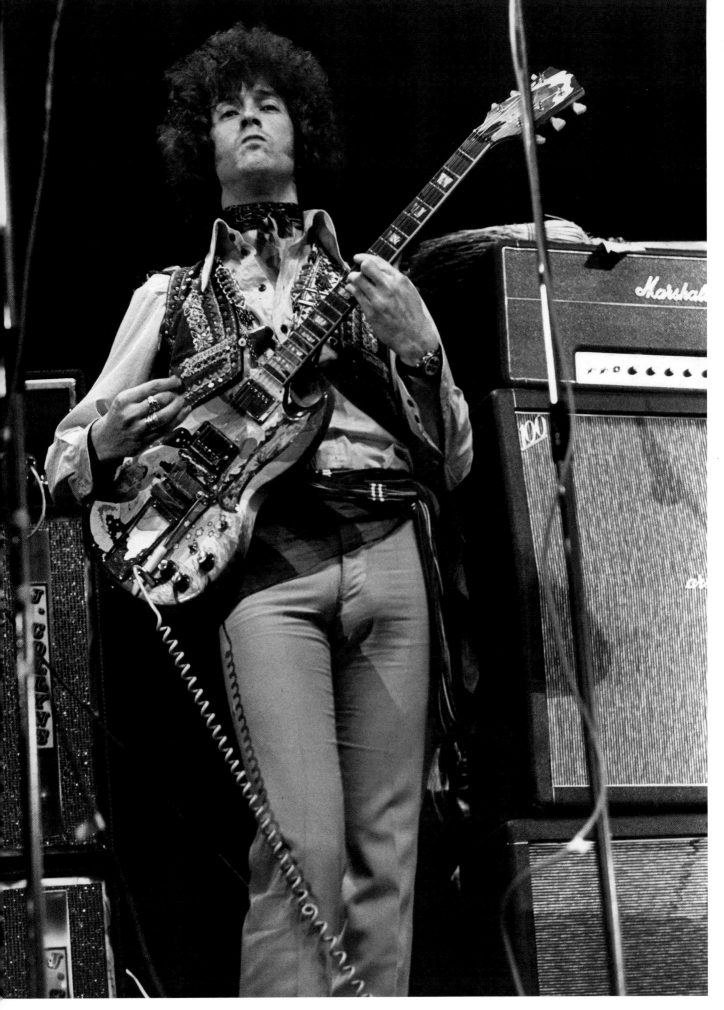

JEFF BECK

Since the 1960s, the names Clapton, Beck, and Page have been uttered in hushed tones as Britain's greatest guitarists. Clapton and Page are easily more famous, but Jeff Beck was a singular virtuoso who took the electric solidbody into realms previously unknown. While he never played actual metal, his first Jeff Beck Group effectively drew up the blueprints—and revealed a heavier path ahead.

With The Yardbirds, Beck (1944-2023) had pioneered concepts of fiery lead guitar and controlled feedback, blues rock, raga rock, and psychedelia, only to be booted out on a 1966 U.S. tour for erratic behavior. Back in London, he cut a few solo 45s for producer Mickie Most (even singing, rather badly, on the bubblegum hit "Hi Ho Silver Lining") before bumping into a singer named Rod Stewart. In short order, they added bassist Ronnie Wood—later guitarist with

AC30 and plexi Marshall JTM45 amps. For about $300, Beck acquired another '59 Les Paul 'burst from future Cheap Trick guitarist Rick Nielsen, this one with rich, tantalizing flametop, all helping define his heavy new rig and tone.

The Jeff Beck Group appeared on the *Truth* LP in 1968—technically billed as a Jeff Beck solo album—and it proved a game-changer, including a '66 session featuring future Led Zeppelin members Page and bassist John Paul Jones, plus drummer Keith Moon from The Who. The result was "Beck's Bolero," a ferocious instrumental laced with Beck's trademark feedback howls and screaming bends. "Shapes of Things" and "You Shook Me" offered relentless heavy blues (sarcastically called *blooze*, for its leaden approach), but the Jeff Beck Group became a hit, especially in the Unit-

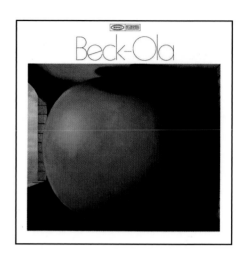

aggressive, as heard in "Plynth." In fact, anyone with a passing knowledge of 1970s metal may hear echoes of this riff in future Deep Purple anthems. Not surprisingly Purple guitarist Ritchie Blackmore has long acknowledged Jeff Beck as his favorite guitarist.

By the end of 1969, the Jeff Beck Group had splintered and Beck was in a serious car accident that took him off the road for a year. By the time he reemerged in 1971, heavy metal had become a bona fide genre, while Beck moved on to funk and soul grooves in the second Jeff Beck Group. His main axe remained a Strat, along with an oxblood '54 Les Paul—a former gold-top that was refinished and converted to humbuckers.

Beck eventually found fame as a jazz-rock solo artist, a career move that propelled his career until his death in January 2023. Still, whenever we hear fierce overdrive and a scorching solo in today's hard rock, we can give a silent nod of thanks for his immortal, proto-metal contributions in the first Jeff Beck Group. ⚡

WHENEVER WE HEAR A SCORCHING SOLO, WE CAN GIVE BECK A NOD OF THANKS.

Faces and The Rolling Stones—and drummer Mick Waller, and the Jeff Beck Group was born.

Putting down the one-pickup Fender Esquire from his Yardbirds stint, Beck scooped up a 1959 (possibly '60) Les Paul Standard similar to those played by Clapton, Michael Bloomfield, and Fleetwood Mac's Peter Green. He stripped its maple top down to a blonde finish and ran the Gibson through a Colorsound Overdriver booster pedal with Vox

ed States where they found a ready audience for their molten thud. In short order, Beck's Les Paul tone and playing became so influential that even Jimi Hendrix attempted to learn the uncanny licks off *Truth*.

For gear, Beck switched things up on the second album, *Beck-Ola*. Instead of a Gibson, he grabbed a '54 Fender Stratocaster, an homage to both Hendrix and his Chicago blues hero, Buddy Guy. The Strat-through-Marshall tone here was even more

JEFF BECK ON *READY, STEADY, GO* IN JUNE 1966.

JIMI HENDRIX

To aspiring guitarists of 1967, the arrival of the Jimi Hendrix Experience's *Are You Experienced* album was equivalent to Martians landing on Earth. Witnessed on his breakout '67 single "Purple Haze," the Seattle guitarist synthesized the blues-rock attack of Jeff Beck, Eric Clapton, and Mike Bloomfield into psychedelia—and upped the game by inserting a relentless funk groove, itself a new music invented by singer James Brown. The single instantly made the young artist one of the most relevant guitarists on the planet.

Born November 27, 1942, Hendrix demonstrated his expertise on three Experience studio albums, the *Band of Gypsys* live LP, and in concerts across four short years. Beyond funk, his rock had powerful roots in R&B—having toured as a sideman with Little Richard and the Isley Brothers only made his playing more credible.

Stone from the Sun"). As a left-handed guitarist, Hendrix found that the Strat was also easier to flip over and restring; remember this was before the widespread availability of lefty instruments. He played other electrics: there are photos of him with a "black beauty" Gibson Les Paul Custom, Flying V, and SG; a Fender Jaguar; and an obscure Acoustic Black Widow. Yet he will forever be identified with large-headstock, four-bolt Strats of the Fender's early CBS era.

Those are just the guitars. His backline mostly comprised Marshall Super Lead 100 stacks for much of his career, though Hendrix endorsed Sunn heads and cabinets and used Vox AC30, Fender, Sound City, and Guild Thunderbass Quantum amps. In addition Hendrix was one of the first players to string together a line of stompboxes, weaving sonic textures with abandon. The stan-

TODAY WE SEE HENDRIX AS THE NEXUS OF MULTIPLE SOUNDS AND STYLES.

Not only was he a blinding soloist, but he was also a whip-sharp rhythm guitarist—something you'd never hear about Clapton or Beck. Hendrix was the complete guitar hero.

Beyond style, Hendrix revolutionized the actual tone of the electric solidbody guitar. Pre-Hendrix, the Fender Stratocaster was rocker Buddy Holly's plank of choice and a California surf staple—think of Dick Dale's reverb-y twang (Hendrix would later immortalize Dale in "Third

dard Hendrix array included a Fuzz Face, Mayer Octavia, Uni-Vibe, and Vox wah, the latter immortalized on "Voodoo Child (Slight Return)." For pristine studio tech, the parade of effects on 1968's "All Along the Watchtower" hasn't been rivaled in over fifty years. One of the most important Hendrix effects of all—the mechanical, spring-loaded vibrato bridge and whammy bar of his Strat—was captured perfectly on "Machine Gun."

As for Hendrix's impact on the evolution of heavy rock, that's incalculable. Young guitarists learned his solos and riffs note for note, though there were precious few who could actually manifest that kind of fretboard fury. Among those who succeeded were John McLaughlin, Eddie Hazel (check the epic solo to "Maggot Brain"), Robin Trower, Frank Zappa ("Muffin Man"), Frank Marino, Pat Travers, and fusion-era Jeff Beck. It would take Stevie Ray Vaughan's arrival in 1983 to produce a definitive heir; even so, Vaughan was wise to go in a wholly different direction, emphasizing Texas blues over psychedelia.

Like Clapton and Beck, Hendrix inspired high-volume musicians without actually playing metal itself. The eardrum-punishing volumes of an Experience concert was evidence of things to come, and Hendrix' expertise at controlling feedback, distortion, and that wild melee of effects all but put *heavy* on the map. Today we see Hendrix as the nexus of multiple sounds and styles, a genuine pioneer—which is why he's regarded as one of the twentieth century's greatest musicians. ⚡

PETE TOWNSHEND

The architects of *loud*, The Who turned up the volume like no band in history. Louder and ruder than its contemporaries, the band cut a swath for acts that would follow: Hendrix, Black Sabbath, MC5, Sex Pistols, AC/DC, Van Halen, Pearl Jam, and more. And guitar giant Pete Townshend was its core.

In a long career, Townshend (born May 19, 1945) has used just about every major solidbody brand and model and inadvertently become one of our greatest amplifier innovators. When High Numbers changed its name to The Who circa 1964, that pale, skinny kid was wrangling Rickenbacker semi-hollowbodies with a backline of Fender or Vox amps. Townshend raged through "My Generation" and "The Kids Are Alright" with a savagery

amps? After playing "My Generation," he smashed a '50s maple-board, sunburst Strat in a plume of smoke and splinters—a tragedy for vintage lovers, but no doubt it launched The Who's career in America.

By '68 the fickle guitar maven began phasing out Fenders for the instrument that would become his staple for the next five years: the Gibson SG Special. One of the great utilitarian solidbodies, the SG Special was fitted with two P-90 single-coil pickups, which might seem odd for a guitarist who made such a racket. Strung with heavy Gibson Sonomatic strings, Townshend made his Specials roar through a variety of fuzzboxes and a rotating back line of Marshall, Sound City L100, and Sunn amps. Crank up 1970's *Live at Leeds* to

electric tone using the most unlikely rig: a '59 Gretsch 6120 Chet Atkins hollowbody and a Fender 3 x 10 Bandmaster amp with an Edwards volume pedal—all gifts from guitar buddy Joe Walsh. Most would think it a great setup for country or rockabilly, but here it proffered the crunchy power chords on "Baba O'Riley," "Won't Get Fooled Again," and "Bargain."

A sea change occurred on the *Quadrophenia* tour in '73 with the arrival of the Gibson Les Paul Deluxe into the Townshend arsenal. For the next decade, the Deluxes and its mini-humbuckers would become his go-to live axes. He had them modified extensively and numbered; the most notable tweak was the occasional addition of a full-sized humbucker between the two minis, an unconventional (yet now admired) configuration.

As for Townshend, it's hard to think of another guitarist who used so many brands and models—from Strats and Teles to Les Pauls and SGs to all manner of Gibson, Rickenbacker, and Gretsch hollowbody and semi-hollowbody designs. Townshend is a true guitar omnivore, as well as a bloody genius of a songwriter and rhythm guitarist. *Who knew?*

HIS CRANKED-UP MARSHALL AMPS PRECIPITATED A REVOLUTION.

hitherto unknown in rock and roll—all the more so when he smashed a few Ricks for onstage thrills.

By the end of '65, the twenty-year-old Townshend got Jim Marshall—the little-known owner of a West London music shop—to build him and The Who bassist John Entwistle early 100-watt heads and big cabinets. These cranked-up Marshall amps precipitated a revolution in live and studio sound, and heavy rock would never be the same. Who can forget the landmark Monterey Pop Festival in June 1967 and the legendary feedback from Townshend's Vox Super Beatle

hear the massive sound of this rig.

When recording the 1969 rock opera *Tommy*, Townshend deployed the SG Special, ES-355, Fender Jazzmaster, Fender Electric XII, and a Gibson J-200 that was his main acoustic for years—listen to "Pinball Wizard" to hear rapid-fire strumming. Around this time, he fully converted to Hiwatt amps for live gigs, notably the CP103 and DR103W, often overdriven by a Univox Super-Fuzz pedal.

In '71 the band recorded another studio masterpiece, *Who's Next*. Here Townshend crafted his signature

PETE TOWNSEND PERFORMS WITH THE WHO, 1971.

THE ROOTS OF METAL

While the first inklings of metal emerged at the very end of the 1960s, its roots went back to the 1950s—and even earlier.

The sound of a high-volume electric guitar came from blues clubs in cities like Chicago, Detroit, and Memphis, where Muddy Waters, Jimmy Reed, Big Bill Broozy, B.B. King, and Howlin' Wolf led bands that pushed the limits of guitars and harmonicas, using small tube amplifiers. T-Bone Walker's 1947 hit "Call It Stormy Monday" is another paradigm-shifting moment. Remember, this is years before the advent of big Marshall-type amplifiers and professional PA systems. Blues clubs became laboratories where music, volume, and stagecraft were mixed, tested, and cranked to perfection.

Many have asked why the sound of electrified rock was simultaneously incubated in the U.S., Great Britain, and Europe. This has much to do with U.S. military personnel stationed overseas after World War II; soldiers and sailors listened to Armed Forces Radio and asked record shops to stock American blues and jazz albums or brought them over themselves. This prompted curious U.K. teenagers to seek out and copy these alluring, dangerous-sounding Chicago blues records—teenagers with surnames like Jagger, Richards, Clapton, Beck, and Page. A 1964 live-television performance by American gospel singer Sister Rosetta Tharpe, seen *wailing* on a white Gibson SG/Les Paul, proved vastly influential on a generation of budding British musicians.

The story of loud continues with Link Wray, the Native American rocker whose late-1950s singles "Rumble" and "Rawhide" were transformative in the development of wild, distorted guitar. Lonnie Mack's singles "Wham" and "Memphis" of 1963 pushed the limits of string bends and fast riffing; James Burton's bending of light, unwound banjo strings on a Fender Telecaster were life-changing, heard on Ricky Nelson's "It's Late." The Kinks' 1964 "You Really Got Me" marked a U.K. turning point, as guitarist Dave Davies put small razor cuts in his amp's speaker to conjure raunchy overdrive.

By '65, the radical "fuzzbox," an electronic pedal that converted clean guitar tone into a square-wave signal, was beginning to transform pop, in tandem with explosive British Invasion. In that year alone, pivotal recordings came from The Yardbirds ("Heart Full of Soul" with Jeff Beck's sitar-like guitar) and The Rolling Stones, with Keith Richards using a Maestro FZ-1 Fuzz-Tone on "(I Can't Get No) Satisfaction." On The Beatles' *Rubber Soul* album, Paul McCartney played fuzz bass on "Think for Yourself."

If '65 was the year of the British Invasion, '66 was the year of British blues and R&B, as The Yardbirds, John Mayall's Bluesbreakers, Ten Years After, and Savoy Brown emerged. The album *Blues Breakers with Eric Clapton* proved to be a milestone on which the twenty-one-year-old guitarist demanded his Marshall tube-amp combo be recorded at shattering levels. This simple act was a Big Bang moment in the history of electric guitar.

Back in America, the Paul Butterfield Blues Band swirled jazz, rock, and blues, inventing the "jam band" concept with long improvisations from guitar aces Michael Bloomfield and Elvin Bishop. Psychedelia, or acid rock, began brewing on the West Coast, deconstructing the pop song in favor of lengthy, hypnotic jams. Guitarists like The Grateful Dead's Jerry Garcia, Jefferson Airplane's Jorma Kaukonen, and Big Brother & The Holding Company's Sam Andrew and James Gurley were critical in the evolution from clean and twangy guitar to loud and fuzz-addled. Bold steps toward hard rock came from noisy bands like Iron Butterfly ("In-A-Gadda-Da-Vida"), Blue Cheer, and Vanilla Fudge, whose smash cover of "You Keep Me Hanging On" influenced everyone from Deep Purple to Led Zeppelin.

By '68 traces of heavy metal could be spied on the horizon, thanks to the bluesy psychedelic sounds of the Jimi Hendrix Experience, the Jeff Beck Group, Jimmy Page's Yardbirds, and Cream. This music itself was *not* metal, but the combination of psychedelia, blues, and Brit-pop pointed toward louder things on the horizon. The parallel arrival of the 100-watt Marshall amp "stack" only confirmed that.

Metal was almost here. ⚡

LEFT: LINK WRAY'S LATE-1950s SINGLES WERE TRANSFORMATIVE IN THE DEVELOPMENT OF WILD, DISTORTED GUITAR.
RIGHT: SISTER ROSETTA THARPE PROVED VASTLY INFLUENTIAL ON A GENERATION OF BUDDING BRITISH MUSICIANS.

PURE METAL

By 1970 the building blocks of heavy metal were in place. The '60s had yielded Clapton and Hendrix, Vanilla Fudge and Iron Butterfly, and the acid rock of Blue Cheer, whose version of "Summertime Blues" reflected America's apocalyptic year of 1968. Led Zeppelin's first two albums arrived the following year, unleashing a rock avalanche that American teens would pay good money for. The industry's label chiefs, A&R staff, promotors, and radio realized the cash bonanza and scrambled to sign the next big band. They understood that metal's business potential was gold—and, in many cases, platinum.

Great Britain birthed many of the best acts—Led Zeppelin, Black Sabbath, Deep Purple, Uriah Heep—but America caught up quickly. Grand Funk Railroad was already among the biggest, baddest bands around and, between 1969 and 1974, landed nine Top 10 records and sold out Shea Stadium faster than The Beatles. Their style blended acid rock, garage, boogie, and Detroit soul, as frontman Mark Farner delivered crude riffery on un-

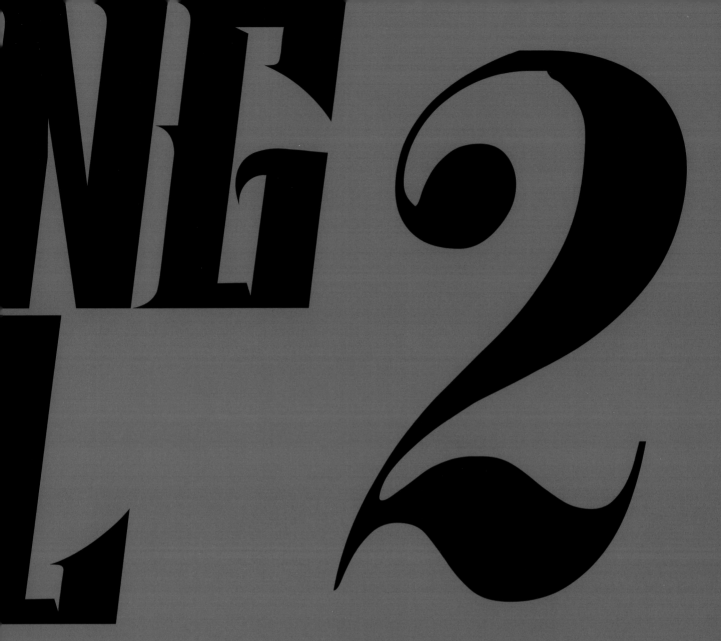

conventional Messenger and Microfrets guitars. His best-known solo was on the '73 single "We're an American Band," but early Grand Funk Railroad is where you'll find Farner's most authentic sludge, such as "Mr. Limousine Driver" and "Paranoid." It was homegrown metal, welded in the USA.

Blue-collar rockers like Cactus, The Frost, The Stooges, and MC5 further carved out the U.S. underground; but for chart-topping action, it's hard to find more accessible FM stompers than Alice Cooper. With lead guitarist Glen Buxton and rhythm man Michael Bruce, the original Cooper band presaged glam with glittery stage clothes and snotty riffs heard on "Under My Wheels" and the hit "I'm Eighteen." Even the eclectic Edgar Winter Group touched on crossover crunch via AM singles like "Frankenstein" and "Free Ride," thanks to flash guitarist Ronnie Montrose.

In the span of just a few years, the genre of heavy metal—which had once terrified adults as a drug-addled teen cult—had become mainstream rock and roll. ⚡

JIMMY PAGE

Guitarists love nothing better than arguing over whether Jimmy Page is a metal guitarist—*or not*. We may never find an answer, but consider this: if Cream, the Jimi Hendrix Experience, the Jeff Beck Group, and The Who primed the hard-rock fuse, Page unquestionably lit the match in 1969. With the release of *Led Zeppelin II* that autumn and its sledgehammer anthems "Whole Lotta Love" and "Heartbreaker," metal was in the air. This rock and roll was neither psychedelia nor blues rock—it was a new beast of fury, electricity, and pure crunch.

The guitars most fans associate with Page (born January 9, 1944) are two Gibson models—the 1959 sunburst Gibson Les Paul Standard and EDS-1275 6/12 doubleneck—but

drums. Multi-tracked guitars and cavernous echo only intensified the sonic assault.

By that fall, the Zep axeman jumped to the '59 Les Paul (bought from Joe Walsh of the James Gang) and a Marshall stack, resulting in a different guitar voice. Page's tone was now bigger and cleaner, offering more power-amp overdrive than throaty fuzz, well heard on "Ramble On." Guitarists like Eric Clapton, Peter Green, and Michael Bloomfield had already shown how the Les Paul, originally designed as a solidbody *jazz* guitar, could conjure a supremely fat tone when coupled to a gain-pumping amp. With *Led Zeppelin II*, Page delivered the coup de grâce.

His '59 Standard (possibly early '60), which Page refers to as "Num-

OVER A HALF-CENTURY LATER WE'RE STILL LISTENING TO AS MUCH ZEPPELIN AS EVER.

the reality is more complex. The first Led Zeppelin album, released in January 1969, was recorded using his Yardbirds-era 1959 Telecaster fed through a Sola Sound Tonebender MKII fuzzbox, wah-wah pedal, and Supro 1690T Coronado amp. The monstrous tone Page achieved on "Dazed and Confused" alone indicated new stylistic trends, abetted by John Paul Jones's heavily compressed bass, Robert Plant's vocals, and John Bonham's pummeling

ber 1," has a 2"-thick mahogany body and a glued-on maple top with a neck of the same tonewood and 22 fret rosewood fingerboard (Les Paul Customs, meanwhile, are all mahogany with an ebony fingerboard.). Page later bought a second Les Paul 'burst, known as "Number 2." Coupled with a shorter 24.75" scale and noise-canceling humbucker pickups, the Gibson design provides a deep tonal persona in contrast to brighter Strats and Teles using Fender's 25.5" scale.

In the studio, Page deployed other electrics too. On the iconic "Stairway to Heaven," you hear that Telecaster for the solo and electric Fender XII 12-string for ringing chords; instead of a Marshall head and cab, the diminutive Supro. On later Zep albums, like *Houses of the Holy* and *Presence*, many of those chiming tones emanate from a blue 1964 Stratocaster. A budget-priced '59 Danelectro was used for open tunings (like D-A-D-G-A-D), heard on "White Summer/Black Mountain Side," and "Kashmir."

His EDS-1275 6/12 doubleneck, a solidbody weighing around 13 pounds, allowed Page to play electric 12-string in concert and dazzle fans, awed by the instrument's seeming complexity. In future years, Gibson doublenecks could be seen in the hands of Rush's Alex Lifeson and Page's former studio chum, John McLaughlin of the Mahavishnu Orchestra, both obviously inspired by Page's onstage innovations.

Metal or not, Page's guitar playing and tone through the '70s was as influential to players of that era as Hendrix and Clapton had been upon '60s guitarists. One could argue it's the most important guitar benchmark of the early decade. As proof, over a half-century later we're all still listening to as much Led Zeppelin as ever. ⚡

FANS PERHAPS MOST ASSOCIATE JIMMY PAGE WITH A SUNBURST 1959 LES PAUL.

TONY IOMMI

If heavy metal was born of psyche-delia and blues-rock, then its first genuine guitar master was Tony Iommi. Emerging in the early '70s with Black Sabbath, here was a musician who was 100 percent metal, inventing acid-addled riffs and slabs of blues-injected leads for the teenage masses. Iommi's three-note riff on "Black Sabbath" from their 1970 debut—with its demonic tritone (flat 5th) note—marks the detonation point. It's a defining moment where we can say metal begins.

Another factor that separates Iommi from other heavy guitarists of the era is, oddly enough, consis-tency. Iommi has rarely strayed from the basic concept of thick, minor-key themes, power chords, and leads. There's little doubt that he absorbed the sounds of Cream, Jimi Hendrix, the Jeff Beck Group, and Led Zeppe-lin, but Iommi (born February 19, 1948) distilled it into a brilliantly simple formula—there's no vague acid-rock jamming or aimless noodling. The music of Sabbath is crisply arranged and stripped to its essence: cue up "The Wizard" to hear an economy of notes, with an emphasis on repetition of the riff. If you want to uncover the secret of Black Sabbath's success, the notions of simplicity and repeti-tion are critical.

Then there's Iommi's mountain of hyper-overdriven tone, paired with Geezer Butler's massive bass and Bill Ward's drumming, which together created the bedrock for Ozzy Osbourne's chilling vocals. Iommi's typical rig included a lefty Gibson SG Special, Laney tube-amp stacks, a Dallas Rangemaster Treble Booster, and a Tycobrahe wah, all

concocting a sound of pure menace and distortion.

Where did that sonic blast come from? Certainly, its members' up-bringing in the bleak industrial city of Birmingham, England, created an edge in the music. When Black Sab-bath entered Regent Sound Studio on October 16, 1969, they ran through their standard concert set, with min-imal overdubs. That first album was mostly recorded in a day, yet marks a paradigm shift in heaviness.

By the release of its followup, *Paranoid*, on September 18, 1970 (the same day Jimi Hendrix died), metal was a living, breathing reality. The rock universe had already witnessed the first two Led Zeppelin albums, Deep Purple's breakthrough *In Rock*, and Mountain's "Mississippi Queen." As Iommi described Sabbath's hum-ble recording approach to the author, "'Paranoid' and 'Iron Man' were cut with just a mic in front of the speaker cabinet. I mean, the studio we cut tracks in was very tiny, so there was

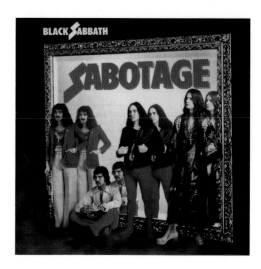

recording of all time, encapsulating the entire genre in a few minutes. He managed to do all this without fingertips on his right fretting hand due to an industrial accident (he uses plastic caps on this fingers), as well as control the hum of single-coil pickups on his SG Specials, notably the '65 axe called "Monkey." Later he upgraded to custom John Birch and JayDee SG-style solidbodies with

HE MANAGED TO DO ALL THIS WITHOUT FINGERTIPS ON HIS RIGHT FRETTING HAND...

no room to put a mic anywhere else. We recorded live, so we just turned the cabinet around, put a mic in front, and played. That's really it."

Iommi's catalog of metallic masterpieces stretches across the void, from "Sweet Leaf" to his out-of-tune G string on "Snowblind," to the Euro-metal assault of "Heaven and Hell." Yet the slow crush of "War Pigs" may be the greatest metal

full humbuckers and 24-fret designs.

The fact remains that when the term "heavy metal" is mentioned, Black Sabbath is bound to come up. It would be historically inaccurate to say they single-handedly *invented* this style of rock, but the Birming-ham band's role in defining it is beyond argument. Sabbath is the de-finitive metal band—and Tony Iommi its ultimate guitar hero. ⚡

TONY IOMMI WITH HIS JAYDEE GUITAR KNOWN AS "OLD BOY," LONDON, 2007.

RITCHIE BLACKMORE

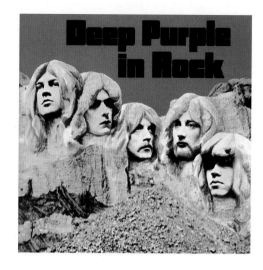

The earliest Deep Purple albums showcased a band exploring high-volume blues and R&B, but all that changed on 1970's *In Rock* album, as the British quintet delivered a molten manifesto. Here the band announced its heavy metal intentions—and never looked back.

At the same time, guitarist Ritchie Blackmore (born April 14, 1945) decommissioned his Gibson ES-335 semi-hollowbody guitar in favor of a Fender Stratocaster—a gift from Eric Clapton—heard vividly on the intro to "Speed King" with insane whammy drops and feedback. Possessing the frenetic speed of Alvin Lee, Blackmore's move to Fenders—echoing his hero Jeff Beck—completely energized the band, heard in "Child in Time" and its magnificent solo.

As Blackmore himself told the author of his guitar influences, "Les Paul was a hero of mine, but there

Country music was in the major keys, whereas I would improvise mostly in minor scales."

Deep Purple broke through to a global audience on their über-work, 1972's *Machine Head*. The powerful roar one hears there is the critical mass of Blackmore's guitar, Roger Glover's bass, and Jon Lord's massively distorted Hammond organ (like Blackmore, Lord pumped his Hammond through Marshall stacks). Together, the combined efforts of Blackmore, Glover, and Lord created that classic thud heard on "Highway Star," "Space Truckin'," and "Smoke on the Water."

For solidbodies, Blackmore was using CBS-era models with big headstocks and maple fingerboards, while in his later Rainbow years, he converted to scalloped rosewood fingerboards. He used only the neck and bridge single-coil pickups—the middle pickup was screwed as low as

the factory with an added output stage, thereby increasing the volume, and the EQ was specially voiced. Blackmore was also fond of Vox AC30 amps for their warm, natural, and dirty tone. He has alluded to using Vox guts hidden in a Marshall housing onstage and then slaving it to a Marshall head—in effect, using an AC30 preamp to fuel the Major's power amp and cabinets.

On the studio solo to "Smoke on the Water" you can hear the Vox combo, with a Hornby Skewes treble booster, while the famous three-chord riff was a distance-miked Marshall, creating that enormous tone. After 1974 Blackmore used an Aiwa reel-to-reel tape recorder as a preamp to drive the amps—remember, this is before amps came with master-volume amp controls (introduced by Marshall around 1975). Instead, various boosters, preamps, wah pedals, and fuzzboxes were used to create the overdriven textures that Blackmore and so many others loud players favored.

Today it's easy to hear how Blackmore's riffs became the foundation for much future metal, including the headbanging '80s anthems of Judas Priest, Whitesnake, Dokken, Dio, and Iron Maiden. When it comes to dark Euro-metal using minor keys, exotic modes, and terrifying Fender tones—Blackmore be thy name. ⚡

BLACKMORE'S MOVE TO FENDERS— ECHOING HIS HERO JEFF BECK— COMPLETELY ENERGIZED THE BAND.

were lots of country players back then who were incredibly fast: Jimmy Bryant, Chet Atkins, Cliff Gallup, Scotty Moore, Glen Campbell, and guitarists whose names I didn't even know. I'd see them on television shows and they were amazing. However, their style was country; mine was more rock and classical.

possible so it wouldn't interfere with his quick picking. To hear his metallic Strat attack, listen to Blackmore blaze on 1974's "Burn."

On tour Blackmore plugged his untamed Strats into a 200-watt Marshall Major head and two cabinets (with another stack as a backup). The Marshall had been modded at

RITCHIE BLACKMORE WITH DEEP PURPLE AND ONE OF HIS CBS-ERA STRATOCASTERS.

LESLIE WEST

In that thundering first wave of hard rock guitarists, there was probably no more important American contributor than Leslie West. With his single-cutaway Gibson Les Paul Junior, the twenty-four-year-old guitarist shook the August '69 stage at Woodstock as a member of Mountain—it was only their *third* concert as a band. While British acts like Led Zeppelin and the Jeff Beck Group dominated the fledgling heavy scene, Mountain put fans and critics on notice that U.S. artists were catching up fast.

In early 1970 Mountain released its biggest FM hit, "Mississippi Queen," a modified I-IV-V blues led by West's vocals, distorted chord chunks, and tube-saturated leads. A key part of their formula was bassist/singer Felix Pappalardi—a classically trained musician who had been Cream's studio engineer and knew how to translate loud guitar tones to tape, long before

style into the FM era, emphasizing bends, sustain, and an authoritative wrist vibrato throughout the *Mountain Climbing* album. In "Theme for an Imaginary Western"—actually written by Cream bassist Jack Bruce—the duo arranged what might be the first power ballad, combining ballad form and Pappalardi's sensitive vocal with gargantuan distorted chords, Hammond organ, and a soul-stirring guitar solo. Jams like "Never in My Life" and "Silver Paper" only confirmed Mountain's metallic might.

For gear, the essential West tone was a Les Paul Junior—a budget student model—plugged into a Sunn Coliseum PA amp and cabinets. It was a four-channel tube head that had been customized; here, the preamps all cascaded into one channel, driving West's vast sustain and overdrive, as on 1971's "Nantucket Sleighride (For Owen Coffin)." Another cut, "Travelin'

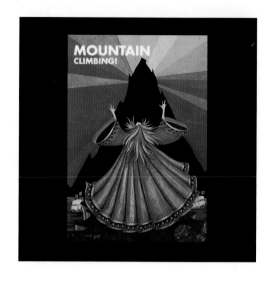

Internal strife forced the group to disband by early 1972, but West rebounded by joining ex-Cream bassist Jack Bruce in a new power trio, West, Bruce & Laing. They toured and recorded two inconsistent LPs, but "Why Dontcha" continued the Mountain mystique. In 1974 Mountain reformed with West grabbing a Gibson Flying V for the tour, modded with a P-90 pickup in the bridge. The new lineup didn't last, and by mid-decade, the outfit was largely relegated to the scrap heap of history—or so you would think.

Over the decades, more and more guitarists keep coming out of the woodwork, raving about West and his enormous influence on hard-rock guitar. Artists like Ozzy Osbourne, Michael Schenker, and Zakk Wylde all cite Mountain's impact, making fans reevaluate a band that, forty years ago, was considered a minor footnote to the Woodstock era. Today we know better: Mountain was a critical band of early hard rock, and its guitarist one of its definitive pioneers. Other than Clapton, no axeman had a bigger tone than Leslie West. ⚡

MOUNTAIN WAS A CRITICAL BAND OF EARLY HARD ROCK AND WEST ONE OF ITS PIONEERS.

that was a common skill. With its signature cowbell intro, West's crunch-fuzz chords, and woman-tone licks, "Mississippi Queen" leapt out of radio speakers, making stars of both Mountain *and* Leslie West.

In contrast to the frenetic speed of Jimmy Page, West (1945–2020) was a stone-cold Eric Clapton freak and brought Slowhand's tasty blues-scale

in the Dark (For E.M.P.)," inadvertently helped kick off the progressive hard-rock sound, combining Led Zep guitar blasts with prog organ and triumphant classical themes. Conversely their uproarious take on Chuck Berry's "Roll Over Beethoven," from a Fillmore East live recording in New York City, captured Mountain in crowd-pleasing boogie mode.

⚡ MARTIN BARRE

In the vast category of underrated guitarists, the name Martin Barre frequently bubbles to the top. A member of Jethro Tull for forty years, he carved out a ferocious body of work during the band's heyday. But compared to an Eric Clapton or Jimmy Page, Barre isn't a household word, despite muscular guitarmanship all over radio and concert stages. Tull's theatrical frontman/flutist Ian Anderson, dressed as a mischievous Elizabethan minstrel, drew the limelight, leaving Barre to rock quietly on stage left. Don't let that fool you—the unassuming guitarist dropped some of the heaviest British riffs of the era.

After three years exploring blues, acid rock, moody jazz, and a smattering of classical ideas ("Bourée"), Jethro Tull took a hard turn on 1971's *Aqualung*, offering a punchy mix of progressive, hard rock, and English

backed it up with relentless touring, which helped Tull crack the States and leap into top-tier status.

Aqualung was recorded at Island Studios in London. Barre recalled those sessions, telling the author, "We had a really hard time making those songs. The studio kept breaking down, and you would think that was a recipe for disaster; but out of all that tension came the most important work of Jethro Tull. There was no concept of acceptance or success at the time; we just breathed a great sigh of relief when it was finished. It was our first recording that brought electric and acoustic songs together, and that set Tull apart from most other bands."

"My God" is a revealing example of the Tull formula, with Anderson's acoustic intro matched with eerie vocals and quasibaroque piano. It set up a theme for Barre's Les Paul

to the power-chord punch of 1975's "Minstrel in the Gallery," where Barre used a '59 Les Paul Standard. Anderson offered a folksy, antipunk statement on 1977's *Songs from the Wood* album, where Barre deployed overdrive and flanger effects on "Hunting Girl" and menacing echo on "Pibroch (Cap in Hand)."

The *Bursting Out* live album of 1978 became a chapter-closing document for Jethro Tull; Barre's thrilling solo on "Aqualung" may have even outshredded the fiery original. Cranking a bevy of Marshall amps, his trademark solidbody at this time was a rising Gibson killer: the Hamer Sunburst, a two-humbucker, double-cutaway with a fast neck and upper-fret access. (Not surprisingly, Barre later gravitated to Paul Reed Smith solidbodies.)

Looking back on Barre's contributions, he remains a much-loved figure, not just for his formidable playing but also for his humble, non–rock star image. In an era of fashionable, even pretty, guitar heroes, the balding Barre proved that a regular bloke could get onstage, plug into a Marshall, and blow the roof off. He's the everyman of dirty guitar—and an essential part of that rock and roll institution called Jethro Tull. ⚡

BARRE IS THE EVERYMAN OF DIRTY GUITAR—AND AN ESSENTIAL PART OF ROCK AND ROLL.

folk music (partly inspired by U.K. artists like Davy Graham, Fairport Convention, and Pentangle). With FM radio exploding across the United States, the album's bare-knuckled tracks balanced Anderson's crisp acoustic guitar and flute with Barre's electric crunch. It was a perfect fit for the format, heard on the ubiquitous title cut, "Cross-Eyed Mary," and "Locomotive Breath." The band

Junior-through-Hiwatt riffing (using a Hornby-Skewes treble booster) and echo-fueled leads. Finally Anderson's jazz-based flute solo clinches the deal, making for a superior radio treat—in hindsight, there's almost no way Jethro Tull could have failed in the early '70s.

The parade of radio cuts continued throughout the decade, from the AM hit single "Bungle in the Jungle"

MARTIN BARRE AND IAN ANDERSON OF JETHRO TULL ONSTAGE IN THE NETHERLANDS.

MICK BOX

Early hard-rock bands emerged left and right during the period 1968–1970: Black Sabbath in Birmingham, England; Mountain in the New York City area; Grand Funk Railroad in Detroit; and both Led Zeppelin and Uriah Heep in greater London. The latter band drew influence from Vanilla Fudge to create their signature power-organ attack, along with chunky bass, guitar, and drums. Though they never achieved mass fame, of all the genre's earliest acts, Uriah Heep is the one that's survived longest—they've recorded and toured continuously since 1969, led by founding guitarist Mick Box.

Given the band's longevity, Box (born June 9, 1947) offers sharp perspective on the dawn of two-fisted rock. He told the author, "When Heep came on the scene, there was only *good music* or *bad music*—categories like hard rock and heavy metal were

today's market. I guess if you had to give our music a name, it would fall under the banner of 'hard rock'; and the one band that most influenced us was Vanilla Fudge. We especially liked Mark Stein's Hammond organ, the dynamics of their arrangements, and vibrato in the vocals."

Much like Deep Purple, their closest kindred spirit, the quintessential Heep sound fused dramatic, minor-key firecrackers with austere ballads, such as 1972's "The Wizard," featuring David Byron's operatic howl and lilting drop-D acoustic guitar from keyboardist/guitarist Ken Hensley. Otherwise, Box's electric maelstrom dominated their sound, created using a black Gibson SG, "black beauty" Les Paul Custom, and Melody Maker with humbuckers— through a ubiquitous wah pedal.

Of those vintage-era axes, he recalls, "The 'black beauty' was sto-

on tour in America we were given these Acoustic heads and speakers, and they were transistor. At first, the amps sounded really good; but that didn't last long and, unfortunately, we didn't have a good backup system in place. So they were phased out, and I was back on a Marshall."

Uriah Heep may have lacked Deep Purple's instrumental virtuosity and knack for writing radio hits, but their fierce boogie and ballad approach earned a live following that's sustained until this day. Box wasn't a flashy soloist like Ritchie Blackmore or Tony Iommi; he plied his trade with riffs, wah-wah screams, and power chords. Box further locked in with Hensley's Hammond organ parts and Gary Thain's bass (a key facet of their attack) for maximum groove. From their 1973 *Live* album, check out the intro of "July Morning" or pummeling crowd-pleasers like "Sweet Lorraine" and "Easy Livin'."

Even a half-century later, it's formidable stuff. ⚡

BOX WASN'T A FLASHY SOLOIST ... HE PLIED HIS TRADE WITH RIFFS, WAH-WAH SCREAMS, AND POWER CHORDS.

invented by journalists who wanted to pigeonhole everything. To prove the point, one of our 1973 shows in America featured Uriah Heep headlining with ZZ Top *and* Earth, Wind & Fire supporting us. You would never get that type of musical mix in

len from Jacob Studios in England when we were recording the *Equator* album. I had to sell the Gibson SG and the Melody Maker when times were a little hard, but they went to close friends. For amps, I was a Marshall man back then; but then

ROCK AND A HARD PLACE

By 1973 the sound of heavy rock and roll was a breakout success, as thousands of teenaged, often suburban, fans packed American arenas to see the latest chart-toppers. On May 5 of that year, Led Zeppelin played a concert in Tampa, Florida, for 56,800 fans, breaking the Beatles' single-concert attendance record and grossing $309,000. The numbers spoke for themselves—hard rock and metal were big business.

The actual guitar business was picking up speed too. Aspiring players could now buy *Guitar Player* magazine, reading interviews with working artists and learning about the intricacies of equipment. With few exceptions, the *solidbody* electric guitar was emerging as the axe of choice, with Fender's Stratocaster and Telecaster and Gibson's Les Paul and SG serving as the gold standards of six-string rockin'. Simultaneously a vintage market emerged for the best 1950s and '60s models of these guitars. That Jimmy Page, Duane Allman, and many other guitar heroes used 1958–1960 Les Paul Standard 'bursts, coupled with the fact that Gibson no longer manufactured that specific kind of flamed maple top, made vintage models all the more desirable—and prices shot up accordingly.

Young players could also increasingly buy effects pedals—the beloved "stompboxes"—to add more sonic colors without much of an investment. Electro-Harmonix debuted its wildly successful Big Muff Pi fuzz and various phase shifters, while MXR brought out the Distortion+, Phase 90, and other boldly colored units. Wah-wah pedals, such as those made by Vox and Morley, had also become *de rigueur* for the modern rocker. More adventurous players could buy ring modulators, envelope filters, and talk boxes to explore tones unknown.

The hard rock phenomenon finally conquered the charts with Led Zeppelin's mega-hit "Stairway to Heaven" and Deep Purple's "Smoke On the Water," proving the sound of heavy guitar was a force to be reckoned with. It was the sound of the '70s. ⚡

JOE WALSH

Jimi Hendrix was a pioneering rhythm guitarist, and, before his arrival, there was no such thing as funk guitar in rock circles. In fact most players were mystified by the technique. Yet one humble player from Ohio figured it out and strutted his funk on the 1970 James Gang hit "Funk #49." That guy was Joe Walsh. Spanking a Telecaster through a '60 blackface Fender Champ, he displayed R&B bona fides in just few minutes of virtuosic grooveman-ship—and Walsh was just getting warmed up. Throughout a long and platinum-encrusted career, Walsh has balanced deep pockets with hard-rock guitar tones, skirting genres and stay-ing on top of the charts.

With the James Gang, Barnstorm, and as a solo artist, Walsh (born November 20, 1947) spent the first half of the 1970s solidifying his place as a fresh American guitar hero. His power chords and whammy dives on the 1971

Walsh's best-known track came in 1973 and has long been his signa-ture anthem: "Rocky Mountain Way." The cut offers an absolutely *uncanny* mélange of a piano hooks, heavy chords, slide guitar, talk box effect, and Arp synthesizer—all with Joe's trademark nasally vocals out front. The kitchen-sink approach worked, and the kick-ass single has been an FM radio staple ever since.

By this time, Walsh had become closely identified with the 1959 Gibson Les Paul 'burst (incidentally, he'd sold Jimmy Page a '59 sunburst, which became the Led Zeppelin guitarist's vaunted "Number 1" Les Paul). As for tweaking the guitar's pickups, he told Ward Meeker of *Vintage Guitar Magazine*, "I'd take the covers off. . . . I went back and forth a lot about whether it made any difference or not, and in the end, I decided it did. I also tried screwing the poles all the way

Felder whipped up a storm on the funk-tinged "Life in the Fast Lane," while Joe drizzled heavy bottleneck on "Victim of Love." Walsh and Felder's dramatic duel at the end of "Hotel California" remains one of the most loved guitar moments in rock and roll history.

Not long after, Walsh added another notch to his solo career with the epic "Life's Been Good," dis-playing more of the economy, crisp rhythm work, and tasty playing that remain his guitar hallmarks. Be-sides touring with The Eagles, Walsh joined his brother-in-law's band and found continued success—of course, his brother-in-law happens to be Ringo Starr, and the guitarist plays a key role in his All-Starr Band.

As a guitarist, Walsh has it all: a stellar reputation at putting the right notes in the right place and a knack for slipping hard-rock textures into radio-ready anthems. Even if you don't own any Joe Walsh albums, you've only heard his guitar playing on the radio *a million* times. ⚡

WALSH HAS A KNACK FOR SLIPPING HARD-ROCK TEXTURES INTO RADIO-READY ANTHEMS.

track "Walk Away" dazzled listeners still mourning the sudden death of Hendrix, the acknowledged master of the Stratocaster tremolo bar. Walsh deciphered Hendrix's secret mojo of trem and feedback long before it was common knowledge. Proving his met-tle, the guitarman straddled hard rock and funk on the track "The Bomber," as well as deploying another secret weapon technique: slide guitar.

down and bringing the pickup as close to the strings as I could—just a quar-ter-turn below where it would cause the string to ring."

Destined for stardom, Walsh landed the co-lead guitar seat in The Eagles and appeared on their 1976 blockbuster *Hotel California*, which fused genteel West Coast harmonies and edgy lyrics with heavy guitar ac-cents. Walsh and guitar partner Don

JOHNNY WINTER

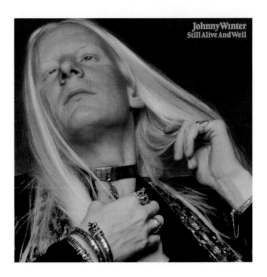

Johnny Winter
Still Alive And Well

Ask any guitar fan what genre of music Johnny Winter played and the answer will invariably be some variant of the blues. But for the first half of the 1970s, Winter was at the apex of American hard rock, adapting his high-speed runs to the cranked-up boogies of the era. From his explosive debut at Woodstock until the Chicago-blues revival with Muddy Waters, Winter was among the fastest, flashiest rockers alive.

Hailing from Beaumont, Texas, Winter (1944–2014) was a regional blues explorer who snagged an unprecedented $600,000 solo deal with Columbia at the end of 1968. His *Johnny Winter* album the next year displayed virtuoso blues rock *sans* psychedelic influences—like The Band, Winter offered American roots music without any fanciful '60s trappings. The sound of slide guitar in rock circles was cutting edge at

come on the scene with everybody telling me how great he was, and I didn't hear it. Johnny overplayed and I was hearing a bunch of mistakes, when all of a sudden, he strapped on the slide guitar, and I said, 'Now I get it!' It was at that point that I realized what Johnny had to offer."

His new band featuring Derringer—the oddly named Johnny Winter And—immediately dove into the FM trend, heard in the opening cut "Guess I'll Go Away." The music was more riff oriented, notably on Derringer's ubiquitous FM anthem, "Rock and Roll Hoochie Koo." The following year's live album had a ferocious cover of The Rolling Stones' "Jumpin' Jack Flash," while 1973 brought the radio favorite "Still Alive and Well," a testament to his recovery from drug addiction. A 1976 concert set, *Captured Live*, marked the end of Winter's hard-rock era. The following

a Dean Johnny Winter Signature, and a headless Lazer travel guitar from builder Mark Erlewine that he favored in later years. A thumbpick was another key part of the Winter attack, as was the section of plumbing pipe he put on his pinky for slide. Amps included models from Fender, Orange, and a 4 x 10 Music Man, while you'll hear phase shifter, Uni-Vibe, and a Boss chorus pedals from time to time.

Reflecting on the hard-rockin' *Johnny Winter* and albums of the early '70s, Winter told Tom Guerra, "I don't particularly care for *those*," infinitely preferring his blues output. "I like *Still Alive and Well*—among the rock records, it's my favorite. The *Johnny Winter* record, that first one for CBS, is definitely one of them; also, the ones with Muddy, especially *Hard Again* and the *Muddy 'Mississippi' Waters Live* are up there."

In declining health, Winter died on July 16, 2014, leaving a huge hole in many rock and blues guitarists' hearts. A humble man who lived a hard life on the road, Winter summed up, "I'd like to be remembered for my work with Muddy—definitely some of the best moments of my career." ⚡

WINTER ADAPTED HIGH-SPEED RUNS TO THE CRANKED-UP BOOGIES OF THE ERA.

the time: Jesse Ed Davis had only recently begun using the technique with Taj Mahal, while Duane Allman, Mick Taylor, and Ry Cooder were all fresh bottleneckers on the scene. By 1970 Winter's hot playing was as exciting as that of any slide guitarist on Earth.

As Winter's longtime musical partner Rick Derringer told writer Tom Guerra, "The first time I heard Johnny play at the Fillmore East, I wasn't really impressed. He had

year, he began a partnership with blues giant Muddy Waters that yielded several Grammy-winning albums.

Any discussion of Winter's gear covers a lot of ground—he used *a lot* of different guitars, but he's mostly closely associated with Gibson Firebirds, notably a 1964 Firebird V for slide. There was also a Firebird with a replacement Les Paul or SG neck, Fender XII 12-string, Gibson SGs and Les Pauls, National Duolian resonators, an Epiphone Wilshire,

JOE PERRY & BRAD WHITFORD

It's impossible to talk about hard rock without mentioning the quantum influence of Aerosmith, who played a definitive role in the genre's rise. The perfect storm between Led Zeppelin and The Rolling Stones—with ample doses of The Yardbirds and New York Dolls—Aerosmith helped forge the Les Paul-through-Marshall guitar tone of the 1970s and dominated the charts for years.

Originally from New Hampshire and later based in Boston, Aerosmith honed the five-piece concept to stripped-down efficiency—two guitars, bass, drums, and a killer frontman to carry the show. Singer Steven Tyler was the face of the band during their 1974–1977 breakthrough, but it was producer Jack Douglas who took the scrappy New England band and gave them their streamlined studio attack. Blunt and direct, Douglas-produced tracks like "Walk This Way," Sweet Emotion," and "Dream On" simply crushed the FM competition.

Behind Tyler, guitarists Joe Perry and Brad Whitford became best known for their economical riffs and solos. Of the two, Perry got more solos and more visibility, propelling him to guitar-hero status and related magazine worship—though Whitford was just as skilled a six-stringer. While Perry leaned more toward the edgy jabs of Jeff Beck, Whitford deployed cool Eric Clapton vibrato and string bends. Their tandem approach was based mostly on keeping their parts streamlined *and* heavy. A cursory listen to "Sweet Emotion" showcases the formula, a fat rhythm groove with a few dirty, overdriven

power chords piled on top. "Walk This Way" confirms how good they were as rhythm guitarists, something often overlooked.

Perry and Whitford carried their back-to-basics method to their backline and axes. Each had 1959 Gibson Les Pauls 'bursts, Marshall and Fender amps, and wah and overdrive pedals, though Perry is also known for a black Les Paul Custom and array of Stratocasters (including reversed lefty Strats, in homage to Jimi Hendrix). Perry's nod to

builders of the mid-'70s was his endorsement of B. C. Rich solidbodies, appearing onstage with the figured tops of Mockingbirds, a rare doubleneck, and the angular 10-string Bich. Without photographs and advertisements showing Perry riffing on one of their unconventional axes, the B. C. Rich company—still around today—might have never gotten off the ground.

Aerosmith's albums of the era remain essential listening. While Perry and Whitford didn't play on the infa-

mous "Train Kept a Rollin'" session of 1974 (it was secretly Alice Cooper guitarists Dick Wagner and Steve Hunter), their style was codified on LP smashes like *Toys in the Attic* and 1976's *Rocks*. For "Back in the Saddle," Perry used a Fender VI six-string bass to double a menacing bass line with bassist Tom Hamilton, while Whitford added fiery whammy-bar licks. For *Rocks*, Whitford recorded his best-known solos on the hard funk of "Last Child" and—perhaps Aerosmith's most authentic piece of heavy metal—"Nobody's Fault," with scorching wah-wah solos.

Of *Rocks*, Jack Douglas told Ben Yakas of *The Gothamist*, "For me, it's the one record . . . where every element is right and in its place. Every lyric, every key, every sound . . . it was written and conceived and recorded in the same place, in A. Wherehouse in Waltham, [Massachusetts]. So we had the place where they used to rehearse."

In '70s concerts Aerosmith was known for their loud, sloppy, and overtly inebriated performances (which had no impact on ticket sales); but in the studio, Douglas's focused production made the band into a taut, whip-smart machine.

Later Perry and Whitford left the band, only to have a platinum reunion with Tyler in the 1980s; but their '70s material remains critical rock of the era. On March 18, 1978, the band headlined the California Jam II concert, playing to over 350,000 fans—a reminder of how enormously popular Aerosmith was in the golden days of FM hard rock. ⚡

BRIAN MAY

There's no more *British* guitar hero than Brian May, the polished, gentleman rocker of Queen. Like many artists who attain career success, May has a "deep bench" of skills: guitarist, singer, songwriter, performer, and gear innovator. His rock-star looks only embellished the visual drama of Queen, particularly alongside bandmate Freddie Mercury, considered by many the greatest frontman in rock history. Add in some of the biggest hits ever, including "We Are the Champions," "Killer Queen," and "Bohemian Rhapsody," the latter of which sold *millions* of singles—and now has *billions* of streams.

On guitar, May was an unequivocal pioneer. While his roots are straightforward—skiffle, '50s rockabilly, British Invasion and instrumental (especially the ubiquitous Hank Marvin), R&B, and British blues heroes like Eric Clapton, Jeff Beck,

sonic recipe includes a tube Vox AC30 amp, his battery-powered Deacy amp (made by Queen bassist John Deacon), a Dallas Rangemaster treble booster, Foxx phaser, and the Red Special, a homemade electric he built with his father Harold in 1963. As Brian told Mick St. Michael about the Red Special, in the book *Queen in Their Own Words*: "I like a big neck—thick, flat and wide. I lacquered the fingerboard with Rustin's Plastic Coating. The tremolo is interesting in that the arm's made from an old bicycle saddle-bag carrier, the knob at the end is off a knitting needle and the springs are valve springs from an old motorbike."

One defining May performance is "Brighton Rock" from 1974's *Sheer Heart Attack*. A guitar tour de force, May delivers his full suite of chops, from fat rhythm riffs to scorching solos. He deployed Maestro Echoplex

(a secret weapon for many British players), May's tone was far less bright than most guitarists, emphasizing powerful midrange tones and a thick distortion that proved all but impossible to duplicate—much to the frustration of aspiring guitarists.

A 1977 track, "It's Late," used many standard May tricks but also added two-handed tapping—a full six months before anyone heard of a young American named Eddie Van Halen. Conversely his rockabilly influences emerged on the hit "Crazy Little Thing Called Love," while the #1 global hit "Another One Bites the Dust" showed clean funk vamps. But for the heavy rock crowd, most of May's six-string achievements came from 1973 to 1977, a space of just four years during which Queen delivered *six* seminal rock albums before moving toward mellower rock and dance pop.

In hindsight, May was perhaps not fêted as much as a Jimmy Page or Joe Perry, likely because he was so technically advanced and therefore difficult to copy. But he was a one-of-a-kind guitarist in a one-of-a-kind band. As such, May's legacy remains unquestionable.

MAY WAS A ONE-OF-A-KIND GUITARIST IN A ONE-OF-A-KIND BAND.

Jimi Hendrix, and Peter Green—May made them all his own with Queen. On their 1973 debut, the band was already mixing posh glam rock with Led Zeppelin thump on "Ogre Battle." It starts with backward guitar, power riffs, and harmonies, all draped in May's signature crunch tone, which was fully formed on their first album.

Queen II continued the sonic assault with "Father to Son" giving more flesh to May's dirty tone. His

units, set individually to 800 ms and 1600 ms, for the real-time harmonies in the solo section, an unparalleled effect that serves as proof of May's equipment innovations.

The warm, woolly overdrive of his Vox AC30 (plugged into the Normal channel) and custom Deacy amplifier were similarly influential, as May conjured a crunch tone different from the brash Marshall-stack formula of the day. Coupled with that Rangemaster treble booster

ROBIN TROWER

Robin Trower is a textbook example of fans triumphing over rock critics, who for years lambasted the former Procol Harum guitarist as a Jimi Hendrix copyist. Throughout a brilliant solo career, Trower carved a niche as a Stratocaster powerhouse, using Hendrix as a starting point but veering off into a molten, post-psychedelic sound all his own. Having James Dewar, a sensational soul-blues vocalist, and Beatles engineer Geoff Emerick didn't hurt either. By the mid-1970s, the guitarist was routinely earning gold albums and packing arenas thanks to FM airplay for those meticulously crafted LPs.

As a rock figure, Trower is almost an anti–guitar hero. In contrast to the notion of wild musicians leaping about in concert and slashing guitars violently, the ever-calm guitarist (born March 9, 1945) barely moves onstage, letting his fingers do the work. With

AS A ROCK FIGURE, TROWER IS ALMOST AN ANTI–GUITAR HERO.

a large-headstock, CBS-style Strat, stompboxes, and phalanx of 100-watt Marshall heads and cabs, Trower's enormous space-rock assault is the stuff of legend. He further stoked the decade's obsession with electric guitar *sustain* (along with Carlos Santana, Mick Taylor, and the Allman Brothers Band) using sumptuous overdrive and gurgling textures of a Uni-Vibe and an Electro-Harmonix Electric Mistress flanger and, more recently, Fulltone pedals.

Though a member of Procol Harum since 1967 (he joined after they released their biggest hit, "A Whiter Shade of Pale"), Trower began expressing his guitar voice on 1971's "Song for a Dreamer," a Hendrix-tinted ballad with stereo guitar effects. The enchanting "Daydream" from his 1973 solo debut, *Twice Removed from Yesterday*, refined his burgeoning style with atmospheric R&B fills and fat wrist vibrato. One simple tone trick involves guitar strings. As Trower told Martine Ehrenclou in *Rock and Blues Muse*, "I tune *down* a whole step to D [and] . . . use heavy-gauge strings. Really heavy on the top two, but those are the ones that you want to pull out the most sound from, really."

The Trower formula finally came together on the '74 *Bridge of Sighs* album: a giant Stratocaster tone, strong writing, Dewar's smoky

vocals, the "op art" cover theme, and co-production from Procol Harum's Matthew Fisher (producer) and Emerick (engineer). On the opener, "Day of the Eagle," the power trio delivered a high-fidelity experience, one that was guitar-forward with massive rhythm propulsion and Dewar's world-weary vocals. Trower also knew how to use dynamics, moving between high-intensity crunch and sultry slow burn to draw in listeners. In the age of concept albums,

suburban ennui, and swirling progressive sounds, it was the perfect blend. Tracks like the wah-infused "Too Rolling Stoned" and "Bridge of Sighs" were ripe fodder for guitar maniacs and stoners alike.

While Trower can certainly rock hard, his best-loved tracks are churning ballads that allow the nuances of his blues solos and pulsating chords to emerge: "Althea," "For Earth Below," and "Long Misty Days" (1976) are supreme examples. Basic similarities to Hendrix ballads like "Hey Joe" and "Little Wing" can surely be detected, but the English guitarist drew just as much influence from bluesmen Peter Green and B.B. King. And unlike Hendrix, Trower rarely touches a tremolo bar.

Like all great players, Trower developed his trademark tone through a rigorous trial-and-error process over an extended period. He told Brian Holland in *Guitar International*, "It all really started from that very distorted Hubert Sumlin sound and a track by Muddy Waters called 'Still a Fool.' I was always trying to make it, right from the moment I'd heard it, you know, that Howlin' Wolf noise. That's what it developed into." ⚡

DON "BUCK DHARMA" ROESER

BLUE ÖYSTER CULT **CULTÖSAURUS ERECTUS**

Dubbed "the thinking man's hard-rock band," Blue Öyster Cult was one of the first U.S. bands to respond to the first wave of British metal and score a vast following as a result. Their 1976 hit "(Don't Fear) The Reaper" became a rock standard, not just on radio but also in film and television. The band's focal point has always been lead guitarist Don "Buck Dharma" Roeser, whose fleet-fingered solos and riffs became nightly show-stealers on the road.

Hailing from Long Island, New York, Blue Öyster Cult arose in the mid-1970s as something of America's answer to Black Sabbath, sharing a penchant for dark, macabre lyrics. Indeed, BÖC's lyric writing was superior to most heavy bands (often co-written by manager Sandy Pearlman and rock critic Richard Meltzer), avoiding hackneyed party-all-night themes in favor of Gothic tales of death, aliens, drug deals gone wrong, and even one infamous Japanese monster. It was all the

nent of early metal songcraft. Riding on drummer Albert Bouchard's chilling vocal and the sonic thud of Dharma, rhythm guitarist Eric Bloom, keyboardist Allen Lanier, and bassist Joe Bouchard, the track vaulted out of the speakers and put BÖC on the map. Dharma's speedy, echo-fueled solo—variously influenced by Danny Kalb of the Blues Project and Ten Years After's Alvin Lee—only made the group even more explosive.

Joe Bouchard told the author, "BÖC wanted to make great records with great songs, and with Buck Dharma as our lead guitarist, our tracks had solos that wailed as good as anyone else's. I don't think he ever signed a deal with the Devil—Buck is just a great natural player. Also, I became a fast picker on bass from watching him play like blazes for sixteen years!"

The essential Dharma guitar rig was basic but effective. His primary solidbodies were Gibson SG models, including a white three-pickup Cus-

Magazine, "When we started buying equipment, we got Acoustic 260 [heads], which The Doors used, and they were terrible amps for the kind of music we were doing [*laughs*] . . . no distortion or overdrive at all. [Then] we got Marshalls . . . the problem was, if we were opening a three-act show, we'd be right on the 'lip' of the stage, and the Marshalls could deafen you. After that, we used Music Man amps for a while, then some Boogie Mark II heads."

Blue Öyster Cult hit its peak from 1976 to 1981, churning out FM hits almost yearly: the reverb-caked "(Don't Fear) The Reaper," "ETI," "Godzilla," "Burnin' for You," Allen Lanier's "In Thee," and the spine-chilling "Joan Crawford." Onstage the quintet would bring the roof down with their "five-man guitar army," where each member—including the drummer—would rock out with a guitar or bass. The crowd inevitably went wild.

While BÖC never ascended to the very *top* tier of heavy acts, they remained an arena-sized concert headliner in the 1970s and early '80s. That combination of earworm riffs, Gothic lyrics, and Dharma's speed-freaked solos gave audiences a brand of hard rock a notch above the norm. Even today Blue Öyster Cult remains an American metal treasure. ⚡

EARWORM RIFFS, GOTHIC LYRICS, AND SPEEDFREAKED SOLOS . . .

more fitting as Buck Dharma (born November 12, 1947) shared an un-canny resemblance to that master of nineteenth-century Gothic literature, Edgar Allan Poe—right down to the small, tweedy mustache.

Blue Öyster Cult's breakout track was "Cities on Flame with Rock and Roll," a 1972 stomper with a big, simple guitar riff—an essential compo-

tom (unfortunately, later stolen), as well as a circa-1973 Les Paul Deluxe with mini-humbuckers, Stratocasters, and, later, headless Steinbergers. His most unusual plank was the custom Bulestra Vulcan, which fused the dramatic looks of a Gibson Flying V with an Explorer.

For amps, Dharma/Roeser told Willie Moseley of *Vintage Guitar*

RICK DERRINGER

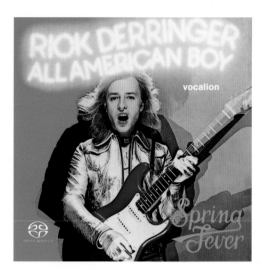

Guitar hero Rick Derringer was *everywhere* in the 1970s. He had already scored a #1 hit in 1965 with "Hang on Sloopy," a garage-rock anthem cut by The McCoys, but five years later, he was working with rising rocker brothers, Johnny and Edgar Winter, both their careers exploding. Derringer's own solo LP, *All American Boy*, released at the end of 1973, unleashed a metallic boogie called "Rock and Roll Hoochie Koo," today a fixture in the classic-rock category. In his spare time, the busy guitarist contributed guitar to '70s and '80s albums by Steely Dan, Meatloaf, Kiss, Barbra Streisand, and even "Weird Al" Yankovic.

Of his influences, Derringer (born August 5, 1947) told *Vintage Guitar Magazine* in 2003, "I grew up listening to a huge variety of music. My folks had a lot of country music, but they had a lot of jazz, too, like the Les

Stones' "Jumpin' Jack Flash" and an incendiary rave on Chuck Berry's "Johnny B. Goode."

Of that era, Derringer told writer-musician Tom Guerra, "I was the kind of guitar player who [grew] up while electric guitar playing was still in its infancy, so I first learned how to play rhythm. This allowed me to be very supportive of Johnny, who was . . . known primarily as a lead guitar player, and frankly, is *not* a rhythm [guitarist]. So our roles became [easily defined due to] the nature of our styles. I took the rhythm place, which a lot of people didn't know how to do the way I could, and this was really the first time that Johnny had a rhythm guitar player. On the other hand, when he gave me a solo, I certainly knew how to take advantage of that opportunity."

Derringer produced the Edgar Winter Group's smash singles

later remake of "Hoochie Koo" as "Jazzy Koo." The fact that Derringer was tagged to record guitar on *three* Steely Dan albums—perhaps the ultimate musician's band—shows how highly his playing was regarded during the era.

For early gear, Derringer plugged a Gibson Les Paul and ES-335 into Marshall amps while a sideman to Johnny Winter. He was also captured on the cover of the *All American Boy* album with a red Stratocaster (a gift from Winter). But the guitar most identify with him is a late-1950s Gibson Explorer with rare split headstock. Later Derringer could be spied sawing away on a highly figured B. C. Rich Mockingbird, as well as PRS and Warrior electrics.

In the subsequent decades, Derringer explored electric blues rock, produced albums for the World Wrestling Federation, and recorded a number of Christian albums. But Derringer will always be best known for his playing with Johnny and Edgar Winter and his own solo efforts. Greatest of all, "Rock and Roll Hoochie Koo" remains an immortal piece of '70s hard rock—years later, the song found a new generation of admirers as part of the popular *Guitar Hero* video game.

THE GUITAR MOST IDENTIFIED WITH [RICK] IS A GIBSON EXPLORER WITH RARE SPLIT HEADSTOCK.

Paul Trio. I grew up loving Wes Montgomery, John Coltrane, and Barney Kessel. I've always looked at myself as a musician first and foremost—and as a singer-songwriter second."

As a member of Johnny Winter And (essentially, the merger of Winter and The McCoys), Derringer produced several albums, including the popular 1971 *Live—Johnny Winter And*, featuring covers of The Rolling

"Frankenstein" and "Free Ride"; later, he launched his own heavy quartet in 1976—Derringer—which tread in the Led Zeppelin and Aerosmith vein. More daring was a 1979 solo album *Guitars and Women*, which revealed New Wave sensibilities and pop eclecticism, also dropping Van Halen–styled acoustic chops in the intro to "Everything." He can also play contemporary jazz, heard in a

THE GUITAR MOST IDENTIFIED WITH RICK DERRINGER IS THIS LATE-1950S GIBSON EXPLORER WITH RARE SPLIT HEADSTOCK.

RONNIE MONTROSE

The late Ronnie Montrose's guitar legacy is one of exciting promise—and unfulfilled dreams. As leader of Montrose, he released one flat-out classic (1973's self-titled debut); but the band experienced frequent personnel changes and broke up in acrimony. Even so, Ronnie's name still carries weight as a formidable hard rocker of that era, as well as fusion explorer and respected sideman.

Montrose (1947–2012) first appeared as a studio guitarist out of the San Francisco area, appearing on two critically lauded Van Morrison releases: 1971's *Tupelo Honey* and the following year's *St. Dominic's Preview*. That's Montrose playing the spritely electric licks on Morrison's R&B masterpiece, "Wild Night," and acoustic lead on the majestic "Listen to the Lion."

Radio listeners got a double dose of Montrose's hot guitar via mega hits with the Edgar Winter Group. On 1973's "Frankenstein," the sounds of

Now a rising six-string property, Ronnie Montrose signed with Warner Bros. and formed the Led Zeppelin–styled quartet Montrose. The album *Montrose* put both Ronnie and his lead singer on the map—future MTV-era frontman Sammy Hagar. With the production team of Ted Templeman and engineer Donn Landee (Doobie Brothers, Van Halen), the album nailed that Les Paul-through-Marshall sound that came to define '70s hard rock. A cover of Elvis Presley's Sun Session staple "Good Rockin' Tonight" became a full-on boogie, replete with Ronnie's power chords and fat blues-scale licks. The rest of the album was full of scorchers: Hagar's tongue-in-cheek vocal to "Rock Candy," "Space Station #5," and crowd-pleasing "Bad Motor Scooter," with Montrose imitating a revved-up motorcycle on his guitar.

While early Montrose was all about that Les Paul and Marshall sound, he later explored all kinds of

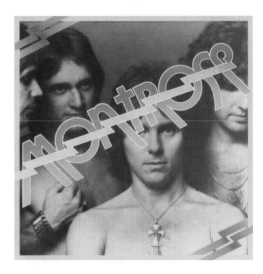

Likely influenced by Jeff Beck's jazz-crossover success, Montrose reemerged in 1978 as a solo artist, exploring instrumental fusion on the album *Open Fire*. The title track was a high-voltage cooker, but Montrose made a bigger dent with his sultry, orchestral cover of the Gene Pitney hit "Town Without Pity," here a melodic showpiece. Montrose's next band was Gamma, a more mainstream outfit that scored modest success with the single "I'm Alive."

In following years, Ronnie's career was punctuated by the occasional solo album and tour, but otherwise his days as a guitar hero dwindled. As he noted, "Musically, I've chosen the path I'm taking, and, for lack of a better term, it's that of an artist as opposed to a craftsman. I've made decisions that were certainly not right in a business sense, but I had to make them; they were necessary for me to survive as an artist. If I feel like going in a certain musical direction, I just do it." ⚡

"IF I FEEL LIKE GOING IN A CERTAIN MUSICAL DIRECTION, I JUST DO IT."

jazz-fusion, prog, funk, and quasimetal were spliced into one instrumental, led by a monster guitar riff and Edgar's Arp 2600 synthesizer. The next single, "Free Ride," launched with Dan Hartman's joyous rhythm guitar vamp, became a Top 10 smash single with a hook you could see for miles. Montrose's hard-rock-over-pop solo put a cherry on the cake.

high-tech tones. His lead on "All I Need" (1975) pushed metal tone with thick, nasally pitch/octave effects. Describing his own playing style to the author, Montrose said, "I'm not really a flashy chops guy; I can play fast, but I don't use a lot of hammer-ons and quick licks. I'm a thematic player and have seasoned more as a melody man than anything else."

⚡ FRANK MARINO

If the DC Comics and Marvel "multiverse" was real, there'd be a timeline where Frank Marino became one of the biggest, baddest guitar superheroes of all time. But in our own humble universe, Marino remains a cult figure, a virtuoso almost too good to play rock—but thankfully he still cranked it up loud with his trio, Mahogany Rush. Even if he never achieved the heights he once seemed destined for, the Canadian's warp-speed picking remains the stuff of legend.

A teen prodigy, Marino (born November 20, 1954) released his first album, *Maxoom*, at the age of seventeen, followed by studio albums that reliably blended hard rock with funk and psychedelia. The guitarist was influenced by Johnny Winter, Robby Krieger of The Doors, and Carlos Santana, but never hid a reverence for Jimi Hendrix, something that

less likely '60s Gibson SG Standards, or dot-neck SG Specials he modified with humbuckers or single-coil pickups. As the musician told *Hit-Channel.com* in 2012, ". . . they call [me a] 'Jimi Hendrix clone.' This guy didn't play a Stratocaster, . . . Marshall, . . . Fuzz Face, . . . never used a Uni-Vibe. . . . I used a transistor amplifier through all the '70s . . . an Acoustic 270 amplifier on my original live album. . . . So, where is the Jimi Hendrix thing? A SG is an easier guitar to play. . . . For me, it's very hard to play Stratocaster because it has a different curvature and when you hang it on your body it sticks over to the right side. . . . For me SG is the best guitar to play when I'm standing up."

The epicenter of Marino's fame was 1978—the year that saw the release of the fabled *Mahogany Rush Live* album, as well as gigging

no easy feat. The album's finale is a cover of Hendrix's "Purple Haze," given the full Marino treatment with savage ferocity and one of his screaming, take-no-prisoners solos.

Neither a particularly strong songwriter nor singer, however, Marino's career waned in the '80s, as rock and roll taste turned toward New Wave, dance beats, and minimalist synthesizers. Still, there are no shortage of contemporary guitarists who credit the Canuck scorcher as an influence, among them, Joe Bonamassa, Eric Gales, and Zakk Wylde—all of whom appreciated those fast blues-scale chops and monstrous tones from his Gibson SGs.

Of his many Gibson axes over the years, Marino waxes most philosophic about an early SG/Les Paul he calls "Old Faithful," described to Willie Mosley of *Vintage Guitar Magazine*: "It's been with me since *Maxoom*. I've done 90 percent of my career with it. I never even changed guitars in the old days—it was this one guitar, all the time, every album, every show. I played it at California Jam 2. It's been beaten, bashed, and fixed. . . . But I still bring it along. It still has its original P.A.F.s. Some people have offered me *a lot* of money for that guitar." ⚡

A TEEN PRODIGY, MARINO RELEASED HIS FIRST ALBUM AT THE AGE OF SEVENTEEN.

dogged his career. Marino's record label even spun a story about young Frank being hospitalized for an LSD overdose and an apparition of Hendrix coming to the teenager in a vision—the absurd tale likely caused more harm than good to the young guitarist's career. Yet it's impossible to hear "Makin' Waves" or "Dragonfly" without noticing the obvious Hendrix connection.

For gear, Marino avoided Hendrix's trademark Stratocaster for

at the California Jam 2 festival for 350,000 fans, sharing the stage with Aerosmith, Foreigner, and Heart. An electric tour de force, the LP captured the guitarist's fretboard fury in covers of "Johnny B. Goode" and the blues staple "I'm a King Bee," which Marino turns into a maelstrom of Mach-speed blues runs, mixed with tasty jazz licks—it's a performance for the ages. Using the vibrato bar of his SG, the guitarist even simulates bottleneck-slide guitar to perfection,

FRANK MARINO CHANGES GUITAR MID-CONCERT AT A MAHOGANY RUSH SHOW IN FLORIDA, 1979.

MICK RALPHS

Bad Company appeared out of the blue in 1974, launching a half-decade domination of FM stations and fan-packed sports arenas. With riff-heavy/sing-along choruses, blues-based guitar figures, and Paul Rodgers' smokey voice, BadCo emerged from the machinations of other bands—Rodgers and drummer Simon Kirke from Free ("All Right Now"), guitarist Mick Ralph from Mott the Hoople ("All the Way from Memphis"), and bassist Boz Burrell from King Crimson. They were also the first act signed to Led Zeppelin's Swan Song label. Zep's rock and roll muscle helped ensure Bad Company's swift ride to the top.

The essential BadCo formula was to simplify the rhythm parts but keep the guitar/bass/drum troika cranked

to talking. I'd got all these songs like 'Can't Get Enough,' 'Movin' On,' 'Ready for Love.' [Mott singer] Ian Hunter, bless him, said, 'I love those songs, but they don't suit my voice,' which I completely understand. But Paul latched onto them, and when he gave his talent to it, they suddenly made a lot of sense to me. It was like back-to-the-blues roots: simplicity, lots of feel—it was a refreshing change to go back to that."

BadCo truly took off when manager Peter Grant made that essential Led Zeppelin connection. With killer songs from Ralphs and Rodgers, Grant's arm-twisting management skills, and the clout of Led Zeppelin, the quartet was a sure-fire hit. In short order, Bad Company trotted out several gold albums: *Bad Company*

Simon were also into blues, so we had common ground, whereas Mott had become a glam band, which was groovy in Britain at the time, but I wanted to get into something simpler—more rock-and-roll, less flashy."

For hardware, Mick's arsenal was as straightforward as the music, preferring Stratocasters, a vintage Les Paul 'burst, and other classic axes, often fed through Ampeg V4 tube amps and the occasional phase shifter. Using a 1957 Fender Esquire tuned to open C for their debut hit "Can't Get Enough," Ralphs knew how to keep things simple, as he told *Music Radar*. "Because [the Esquire] is just one pickup—it's really raunchy—you get more gain out of it. Also, the neck pickup on a Tele has always been a waste of time as far as I'm concerned: it's got no balls to it. I'm not a country picker, really; I like a nice, beefy, raunchy sort of sound. I saw an old clip of Muddy Waters the other day and he was playing an old Fender Esquire. I like the simplicity of it: two knobs, one pickup." ⚡

> **FOR HARDWARE, MICK'S ARSENAL WAS AS STRAIGHTFORWARD AS THE MUSIC, PREFERRING STRATOCASTERS, A VINTAGE LES PAUL 'BURST, AND OTHER CLASSIC AXES.**

to hard-rock perfection, all leaving room for Rodgers' soulful moan. As Mick Ralphs told Jamie Dickson of *Music Radar* in 2011, "I wanted to get back to something more basic and bluesy, so I teamed up with Paul Rodgers . . . he had a band after Free called Peace at the time and we got

(1974), *Straight Shooter* (1975), *Run with the Pack* (1976), through 1979's double-platinum *Desolation Angels*. Compared to Mott the Hoople, Ralphs told Eliot Stephen Cohen in *Vintage Guitar*, Bad Company ". . . was really just more my cup of tea because it was a blues-rock band. Paul and

MICK RALPHS, KEEPING THINGS SIMPLE WITH BAD COMPANY, CIRCA 1975.

Following a decade of boundless experimentation, the balance of power between record companies and artists shifted in the mid-1970s. Chart-topping albums from Bruce Springsteen and Peter Frampton hinted at the immense revenue labels could earn, putting fresh pressure on producers, A&R men, and bands to deliver hit singles and albums. In short order, the ten-minute epics of Led Zeppelin, Yes, ELP, and Jethro Tull disappeared and were replaced by shorter choruses, each artist looking for the catchiest "hook" to grab the listener.

A new generation of guitar-oriented acts arose, each slicker and more craftily packaged than their predecessors: think Boston, Heart, Kansas, Journey, Ted Nugent, Styx, Cheap Trick, and REO Speedwagon. Even The Cars, who managed to take the New Wave fad and blend it with chunky rock riffs, brought their rare hybrid to the top of the charts. Fans responded enthusiastically to this new style, dubbed *arena rock* for the concertgoers who filled hockey and basketball arenas on non-game days. The larger pop market was also expanding and becoming more inclusive; punk rock aside, rock was no longer a social threat. Suburban moms took their tweens to Kiss concerts, as if a genteel family outing.

ARENA
ROCK

Peter Frampton is a useful case study, as he threaded the needle between hard rock and sugary pop with maudlin lyrics, pleasing melodies—and scorching solos on a triple-pickup Les Paul Custom. In 1971 his guitarmanship was heavily featured in the crunch classic, Humble Pie's "I Don't Need No Doctor" (sharing axe duties with the late, great Steve Marriott)—but his breakthrough arrived with *Frampton Comes Alive*, a multiplatinum LP that spun off endless singles. More importantly, Frampton became emblematic of this new alliance between heavy riffing and pop melody. For proof, he played a single June 1976 show at Veterans Stadium in Philadelphia—for over *100,000 fans*.

While his stay at the top of the charts didn't last long, Peter Frampton might well be considered the father of arena rock. ⚡

EDDIE VAN HALEN

When the debut *Van Halen* album arrived in March 1978, the guitar universe was hit by a meteor of seismic force. Eddie Van Halen's two-handed tapping, proto-shred insanity, and whammy trainwrecks had never been heard in hard rock. Jazz-fusion maybe—but good-time FM rock? Absolutely *no one* saw Eddie coming.

The young player's solos and riffs remain legendary, as he splatter-painted notes over a canvas of rock and pop-fueled crunch. Speaking to National Guitar Museum Director H. P. Newquist, Eddie mused, "I think about some of our older stuff, like 'Ain't Talkin' 'bout Love.' People love that song, but it's really just a two-chord song. Billy Gibbons [of ZZ Top] calls me now and then, and he asks, 'Eddie, have you found that fourth chord yet?' You can do stuff like Rush,

style ash body and extra-wide $30 neck. It had extra-large Gibson frets, Schaller tuners and a re-potted PAF pickup from a '61 ES-335. The vibrato bridge was reputedly from a pre-CBS Strat. This is the guitar you heard on the first Van Halen album, apart from an Ibanez Destroyer he called "the Shark" on "You Really Got Me."

Eddie (1955–2020) deployed other legendary axes over the years: "Bumblebee" (a yellow and black super-strat); Frankenstein #2 with a Floyd Rose vibrato and locking nut (red and black super-strat); the Kramer 5150 Baretta; his Steinberger GL2T TransTrem with EMG pickups (mid-'80s era); Music Man EVH; and the Peavey Wolfgang, known today as the HP Special. Later Eddie launched his own EVH brand of guitars and amps. Not even Eric Clapton has his

blades at you or a mature redwood. I like a warm, brown sound—just like my brother's snare drum."

Of his Ernie Ball Music Man signature (now called the EBMM Axis model), Eddie further told the author, "I was looking for something that crossed the classic lines of a Les Paul with a Tele. I also had it in my mind that the guitar should be balanced, not too heavy and somewhat small since I'm not a real big guy. I wanted something that would stand the test of time because most guitars made these days are bastardized Strats."

In summation of his illustrious career, Eddie Van Halen told Newquist, "I'm probably one of the luckiest, most-blessed guys on the planet to be able to do what I do and enjoy it, and have other people like it. To have inspired other people to play an instrument makes me feel good. Kids have to grow up on somebody, just like I grew up on Clapton, there's a whole new generation of guitar fans. If I inspired anyone to pick up a musical instrument, that's great—because that's what it's all about." ⚡

EDDIE INFLUENCED THE GEAR MOST OF US PLAY ... GUITARS, AMPS, AND EFFECTS.

Yes, or U.K.; but that's more *musician's* music. I'm not knocking any of them—I would love to be able to do that kind of music—but my brain is not cut out for it. I like simple things. *Powerful*, simple things."

Eddie's greatest impact on the instrument perhaps wasn't solely his tapping and whammy dives but something closer to home—*guitar gear*. He singlehandedly influenced the equipment most of us play, including guitars, amps, effects, and accessories. Eddie's #1 "Frankenstein" was built with a $50 strat-

complete own line of self-branded gear—that's the enormous cultural power of Eddie Van Halen.

Eddie's original Marshall 100-watt heads included a '67 Super Lead combined with a Variac voltage transformer to lower the volume but preserve the tone—this is the origin of his fabled "Brown Sound." Talking to the author, Eddie discussed his tone on early albums, describing a sound that is big and warm, not trebly and brittle: "I use that term to describe the difference between having someone chucking razor-

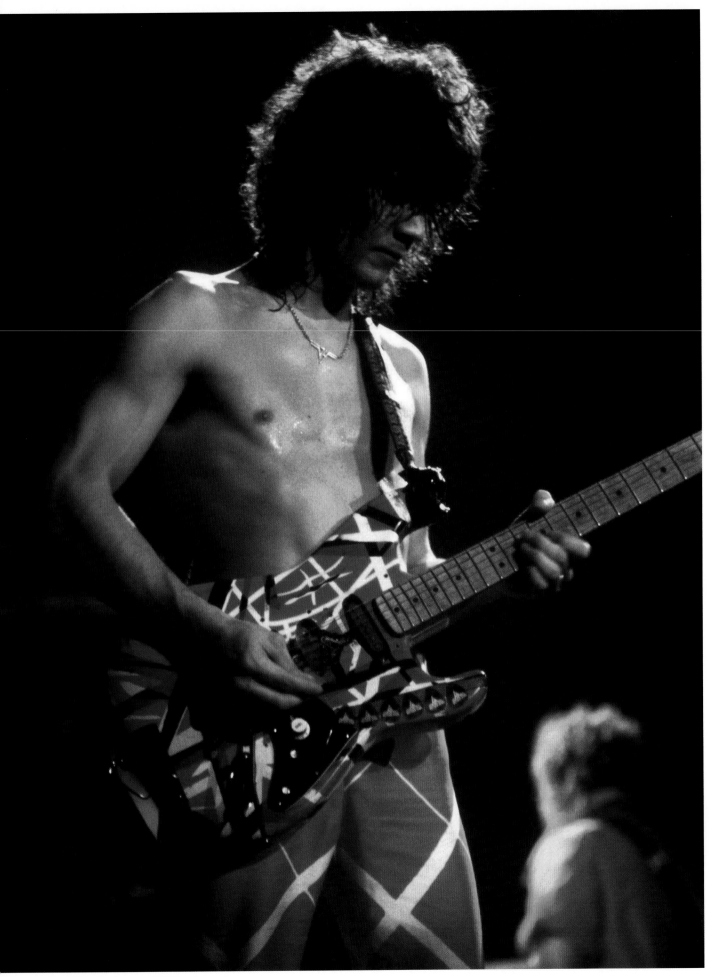

ACE FREHLEY

There was a *brief* moment when Ace Frehley was among the hottest players on the planet. As leadman for Kiss, "the Spaceman" was a comic book hero come to life, peeling off solos with his trademark wobbly vibrato and lighting off smoke-bomb effects from his Les Paul. Along with the rhythm riffs of Paul Stanley, they rocked Kiss stages all over the planet, much to the delight of millions of fans.

Though sometimes derided as a novelty band, Kiss melded hard rock, glam, bubblegum, and Barnum & Bailey into an act that was focused on the live extravaganza—their studio albums were essentially commercials enticing fans to buy tickets. Not surprisingly, their early studio albums aren't remarkably strong, but their first live album was

seen with a pair of 1974 Customs and a '73 Deluxe, all modded with DiMarzio Super Distortion humbuckers. The three-pickup, ebony Custom had only two actual pickups—the neck slot held the smoke-bomb for concert thrills. His pedals were kept to a minimum; video of his guitar solo from a 1976 concert display fuzz, phaser, echo, and octave effects, likely triggered offstage by an engineer or roadie, allowing Frehley to focus on his performance.

As Frehley told the author, "Originally, Paul, Gene, and Peter put an ad in the *Village Voice*, which I answered. After we got a record deal, we designed the makeup and decided to become a theatrical rock group. Live, I had to juggle playing guitar and keeping up with the live show. Our shows

standard EL34s). Paul Stanley used cheaper, Norlin-era Gibsons like the Marauder, S-1, and L6-S as stage props, smashing them onstage to the gleeful roar of fans. Another of his standards was the Ibanez Paul Stanley model, shaped like their Iceman line.

Of his guitar approach, Frehley told the author, "Ninety percent of my studio solos are spontaneous; usually the first take is the one I keep. If there are a couple of bad notes, we'll punch-in some new ones. Earlier in my career, I tried working out solos, but now playing off the top off my head works best. The harmonized lead in 'Detroit Rock City' was worked out, of course, but that was written by Bob Ezrin who produced the *Destroyer* album."

After Kiss, Frehley went on to a modest solo career and later joined a popular Kiss reunion in the 1990s, but his essential work came between 1974 and 1977. This is prime-era Kiss, when the band broke out of New York City and conquered the world. They were only an authentically hard-rock quartet until 1976's pop-infused *Destroyer* and *Rock and Roll Over* albums, but heavy riffing has always been a part of the entertainment behemoth's formula. It's easy to write off Kiss as a less-than-serious act, but in their heyday, Frehley's guitar work was the stuff of legend. ⚡

FREHLEY'S LIVE RIG WAS STONE SIMPLE AND THEREIN LIES ITS BEAUTY.

a game-changer. Released in 1975, *Alive!* proved an essential concert keepsake, reinforcing the idea that everyone should catch the band live. The recording was cleverly doctored in Electric Lady Studios by producer Eddie Kramer (Jimi Hendrix, Led Zeppelin) to simulate a live document. It *wasn't* but it still hit pay-dirt on the charts. To this day, it remains the ultimate Kiss album—and an Ace Frehley tour de force.

Frehley's live rig was stone simple and therein lies its beauty. A diehard advocate of Gibson Les Pauls, the Bronx-born guitarist was often

were pretty well rehearsed, especially the choreography—but there was some improvisation, too."

Kiss's backline was basic enough: a wall of Marshall Super Lead 100-watt heads and a phalanx of 4×12 cabinets, few of which were actually miked onstage. The essentially Ace Frehley tone was a Les Paul plugged into cranked-to-11 Marshalls that were relatively clean. The overdrive crunch you hear comes from sheer volume and the sound of overdriven power tubes doing their job (Frehley reputedly used tighter 6550 power tubes instead of

A DIE-HARD ADVOCATE OF LES PAULS, ACE FREHLEY WAS OFTEN SEEN WITH 1974 CUSTOMS AND A '73 DELUXE.

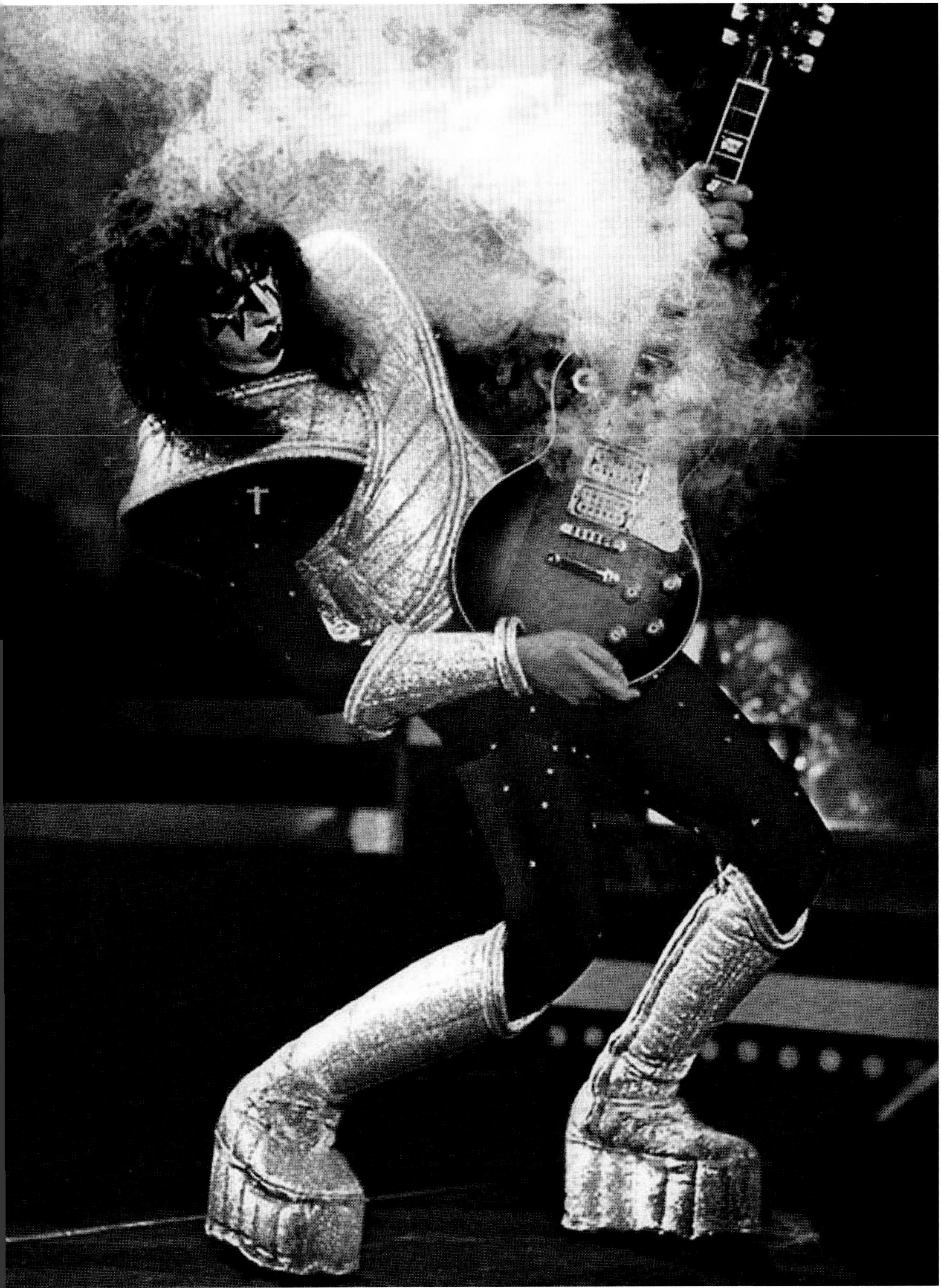

TOM SCHOLZ & BARRY GOUDREAU

One of those "A Star is Born" moments, the arrival of Boston's debut release in August 1976 was a sea change that changed hard rock—and home recording—forever. Crafted in the basement of guitarist Tom Scholz's humble Massachusetts home, the album's sparkling audio quality and tight arrangements raised the bar for musicians, producers, and engineers around the globe. The huge tones of Scholz and co-guitarist Barry Goudreau were just as unprecedented. The quintet struck FM gold with singles like "More Than a Feeling" and "Peace of Mind," and the *Boston* album eventually sold over 17 million copies.

Boston's sonic trademark combined Brad Delp's soaring voice with stacked guitar harmonies—often just Tom Scholz overdubbing himself in his studio. The defining guitar moment from Barry Goudreau

LP of the same name. A barrage of lawsuits and internal feuding led the original Boston lineup to shatter in the early '80s, with Scholz assuming total control of the band. Since then, the rock institution has toured and recorded sporadically, with numerous personnel changes; as a recording band, only their first two albums retain any historical significance.

Outside Boston, the guitarist/studio wizard formed an electronics company called Scholz Research & Development, which created groundbreaking guitar gear like the Rockman, a portable headphone amp delivering realistic amp distortion, chorus, compression, and echo. Its arrival coincided with arrival of portable four-track cassette decks, providing 1980s guitarists a boon in affordable home recording. Another product was the Power Soak, an attenuator that allowed players to

THE HUGE TONES OF SCHOLZ AND CO-GUITARIST GOUDREAU WERE UNPRECEDENTED.

(born November 29, 1951) lies within "Foreplay/Long Time," a grandiose anthem with his razor-toned, Jeff Beck–infused solos over Scholz's Hammond-organ work. Goudreau's slide was also featured on the single "Don't Look Back," from their 1978

turn their amplifier heads louder but lower the volume to practice or record—and, more importantly, derive richer overdrive from the head's preamp and power tubes.

For guitars, Goudreau was typically seen onstage with an SG, while

Tom Scholz has long been associated with Gibson Les Paul goldtops—his most famous one is a 1968 Deluxe with a sanded-down top, bridge humbucker, and P-90 pickup in the neck slot. As he told Ted Drozdowski for Gibson.com, Scholz is devoted to Les Pauls because ". . . they sound great—period. The first time I saw somebody play one was Jimmy Page and then I heard Jeff Beck use one on *Truth*. Then, I heard someone play a goldtop in a bar and I thought it was the sweetest sounding thing. 'Where do you find a guitar like that?' A couple years later, that guy had to sell his equipment and offered me that very guitar for 300 bucks. It's the same one I use today. . . . The sound is big with lots of character . . . if you want a chunky sound it's there, or if you want a pure, crystal clear tone it does that. I just don't get that range from other guitars." ⚡

TOM SCHOLZ AND BARRY GOUDREAU OF BOSTON AT NEW YORK CITY'S MADISON SQUARE GARDEN.

ULTIMATE HEAVY METAL GUITARS

NANCY WILSON

During heavy rock's first decade, the role of guitar player largely remained a male domain. There were powerful women *singers*—Janis Joplin, Grace Slick, and Pat Benatar among them—yet before the '90s grunge era (which kicked open a lot of gender doors), the sight of women playing electric guitars and basses was rare, apart from Sister Rosetta Tharpe, Bonnie Raitt, glam rocker Suzi Quatro, or Fanny's June and Jean Millington.

Heart changed all that.

Hailing from the Pacific Northwest, Heart was led by powerful singer Ann Wilson and sister Nancy Wilson on guitar, scoring breakout hits from 1976 onward and earning fans for their melodic, radio-ready hard rock. The original lineup included electric guitarists Roger Fisher and Howard Leese, with Wilson using either electric solidbodies or an Ovation acoustic-electric at live shows—effectively re-creating the *acoustic-meets-electric* dynamic of one of Heart's biggest influences, Led Zeppelin.

The band's debut, *Dreamboat Annie*, album exploded in early 1976, achieving significant chart action. Heart's Zep pedigree was on full display in their first hit, "Crazy on You," thanks to a deft fingerstyle acoustic intro from Nancy, clearly in a Jimmy Page vein. Despite the Beatles and Led Zeppelin influences, the follow-up hit "Magic Man" was straight out of the Bad Company school of economical, mid-tempo thump—heavy enough to be hard rock but with lighter vocal and synthesizer nuances to bring it to radio's attention. (The Bad Co. connec-

tion proved prescient: post-Heart, guitarist Howard Leese toured with singer Paul Rodgers and eventually became a full-fledged member of Bad Company.)

In 1977 the Wilson sisters returned with the three-time platinum *Little Queen* and its genuinely metal single "Barracuda." The track vaguely resembled Led Zeppelin's "Achilles Last Stand" from the previous year, borrowing a similar driving drum/bass groove and ringing power chords. Subsequent albums found Heart dialing down the guitar distortion for "Straight On" (1978) and New Wave–influenced "Even It Up" (1980), but their career soured in the early '80s as rock tastes changed. The Wilsons reinvented themselves in 1985 as a glam-metal act, delivering MTV power ballads "What About Love," "Never," and Nancy Wilson–sung "These Dreams." Heart was back on top of the charts.

Of her supportive style of guitar playing, Wilson told Johnny Zapp of *Vintage Guitar Magazine*, "With electric, I play with heavy strings. I'm not bending like a lead player; I bend like a rhythm player, inside rhythms, so I think it makes a better sound with heavier strings. It gives more resistance so I can play electric kind of the same way I play acoustic, which is rather aggressively! I play mediums on acoustic because I like to get more of the rich tonality from the strings. I do step out on lead a few times live, but it's not my passion to be a lead player. I think *inside* the songwriting, rhythm, and singing of the song."

Gear-wise, Leese would variously grab a Les Paul, Explorer,

or Telecaster, while Roger Fisher was primarily known for playing a Fender Stratocaster. Over the years, Wilson has used Teles, the Gibson Nighthawk, a Duesenberg Starplayer semi-hollow, and her signature Martin HD-35 dreadnought. Still the definitive Heart guitar is an Ovation acoustic-electric roundback. While Wilson actually used a Guild Jumbo acoustic to record the intro to "Crazy on You," those Ovations—with patented Lyracord backs—are what most associate with her. In early years Wilson toured with both the standard round-soundhole Legend and fancier, non-cutaway Adamas 1687-7 model.

More importantly the vision of Nancy Wilson playing guitar onstage helped kick-start the revolution of women instrumentalists. Her work helped pave way for future rock stars Joan Jett and Lita Ford, The Go-Go's, bassist Tina Weymouth of Talking Heads, The Bangles, Kim Deal of the Pixies and The Breeders, and '90s grunge heroes Hole.

For that alone, Heart should be regarded as a major band. ⚡

THE VISION OF NANCY WILSON PLAYING GUITAR ONSTAGE HELPED KICK-START THE REVOLUTION OF WOMEN INSTRUMENTALISTS.

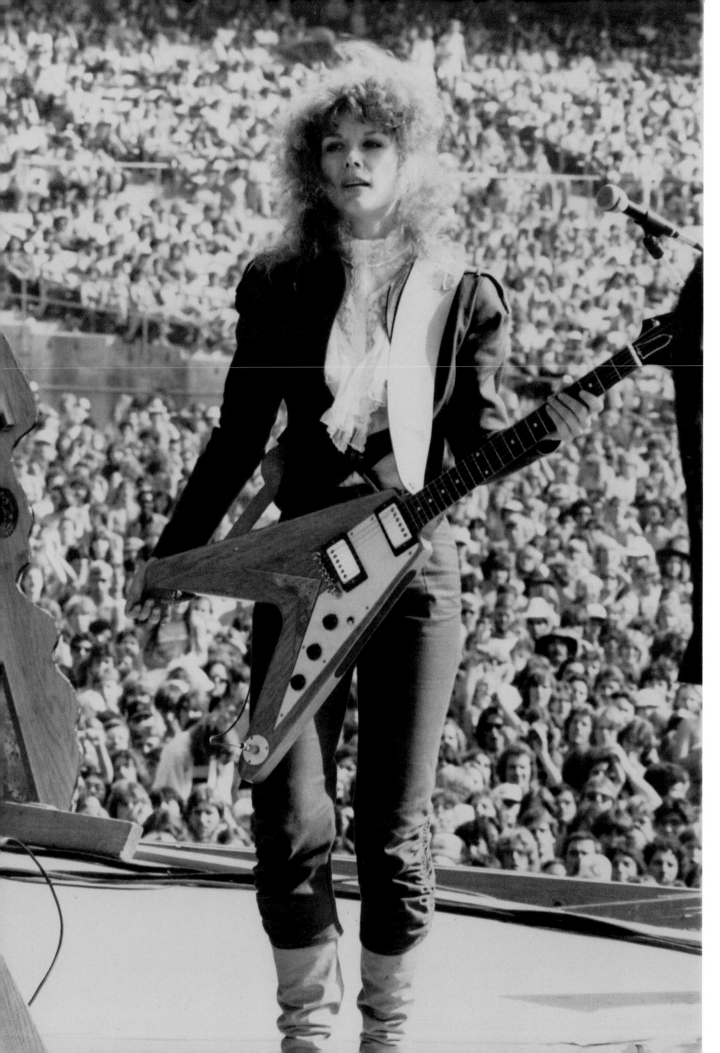

NEAL SCHON

This San Francisco guitarist has enjoyed what one might term a "big career," lasting over 50 years and counting. Neal Schon (born February 27, 1954) became a bona fide guitar hero with platinum-selling Journey, as well as playing with Santana, Bad English, Michael Bolton, Paul Rodgers, synth master Jan Hammer, and on a raft of solo projects. Schon is particularly adept at taking *heavy* guitar tones and embedding them inside pop-oriented songs—he can shred as fast as anyone but also has a knack for melody that has appeared on albums selling millions of copies. Not every guitarist can do that.

The Schon saga began when he was asked to join Eric Clapton's Derek & The Dominos as a teenager. In early '71, around his seventeenth birthday, Schon joined Santana, becoming a guitar foil for Bay Area wizard Carlos Santana. The combina-

quartet became a high-voltage rhythm section, providing a bed for the guitarist's long, fusion-y solos. After octave-leaping vocalist Steve Perry joined in 1977, Journey began pushing in a pop-rock direction for the *Infinity* and *Evolution* albums, Schon dropping bluesy, melodic licks into radio fodder like "Lights," "Wheel in the Sky," and the inane "Lovin', Touchin', Squeezin'." The manner in which Schon could place a fierce, highly distorted lead into a ballad came in no small part from his former boss, Carlos Santana, who perfected the concept in his own "Samba Pa Ti" and "Europa."

On 1980's *Departure*, Schon perfected his method of injecting ferocious guitar into commercial material. The single "Any Way You Want It" is up-tempo hard rock yet also has sweet pop harmonies and tuneful major-key choruses. Within

tapes. Within the music industry, arena rock was now called AOR, standing for *album-oriented rock*, an easy-on-the-ears format that skewed the line between AM pop and FM rock. Along with the Eagles and Fleetwood Mac, Journey was an undisputed master of the category for several years.

Beyond stage and studio heroics, Schon was a serious guitar collector and reflected on his most famous six-string, telling Ward Meeker of *Vintage Guitar Magazine*, "The black Gibson Les Paul Pro, with a Floyd whammy, has been on many famous records and tours: 'Stone in Love,' 'Who's Crying Now,' and the *Escape* tour. What's interesting about that guitar is the fretboard is ebony and the neck is maple, so it's got some snap with the mahogany body—it speaks really well."

Of his electrifying lead style, Schon told the author in 1989, "I like Joe Satriani—*who doesn't?*—but I don't need to go crazy like that on every song because his songs are set up to let him show off in every aspect. Joe's doing all this monster stuff on guitar, but I'm not really from the flash school; I'm more from a blues school. I want to make people realize there are still melodic players in the world."

"I'M NOT REALLY FROM THE FLASH SCHOOL; I'M MORE FROM A BLUES SCHOOL."

tion proved explosive on *Santana III*, as Schon can be heard harmonizing and trading fiery solos with Santana on "No One to Depend On." For the follow-up, 1972's *Caravanserai*, the guitar duo explored the vanguard of Latin jazz-rock fusion.

This Santana lineup splintered after the next tour, creating an opportunity for Schon and keyboardist Gregg Rolie to form their own band, which they dubbed Journey. On their earliest albums, the new

its grooves, Schon takes a madcap solo. Radio quickly jumped on this exciting anthem, and American rock fans gobbled it up.

The pump was thus primed for 1981's *Escape* album and the ensuing superstardom for Journey. With mega-hits like "Don't Stop Believin'," "Who's Crying Now," and six-string inferno of "Stone in Love," *Escape* earned a rare diamond certification, indicating U.S. sales of over 10 million LPs, cassettes, and 8-track

ANGUS & MALCOLM YOUNG

Amid the long and illustrious history of metal, few bands sit as loftily as AC/DC, the Australian quintet that stormed the world with three-chord barnburners like "Back in Black" and "You Shook Me All Night Long." Their music has never been about flash or gimmicks—it's about a tight bass-and-drum beat that never lets up, topped with crisp guitar work, a great vocal, and bawdy lyrics that seal the deal. In their prime, AC/DC's founding brothers Angus and Malcolm Young maintained a kind of ruthless efficiency, never overplaying with too many notes. Malcolm's enormous power chords and Angus's bluesy string bends and vibrato remain the essence of tasty hard rock.

Hailing originally from Scotland, the Young brothers launched AC/DC in the mid-1970s but didn't achieve wide attention until 1979's *Highway to Hell*. Its title track became one of the great rock anthems, an exercise in metal minimalism that hit the listener straight between the eyes with a thundering beat, big chords, and a party-hearty chorus from singer Bon

virtues of stripped-down rock and roll, hoisting a beer, and partying with your mates. Sound familiar?

In contrast to the nimble pyrotechnics of Eddie Van Halen or Neal Schon, Angus Young offered a different kind of guitar ace, prancing onstage in his naughty schoolboy knickers and rocking up a storm with a combination of '50s rock overdrive and British blues licks, à la Eric Clapton and Jimmy Page. As Angus told the German magazine *Guitar*, "When I look at all the players who I admire, there's *a lot* of players. . . . I really got focused on [playing] around the years when I was about 12 into my teenage years; I started to focus more on it. Around when I was about 13 [or] 14, that's when Jimi Hendrix appeared on the horizon, and . . . I first heard the song 'Purple Haze.' . . . When along came Hendrix, you kind of went, '*Woah!* This is another level on guitar.'"

Following the success of *Highway to Hell*, singer Bon Scott died suddenly of alcohol poisoning in 1980—and the band nearly

the Young brothers never lost sight of that monstrous AC/DC groove. Over the next decade, they recorded not only hits but tireless metal classics: "Back in Black," "Shoot to Thrill," "You Shook Me All Night Long," "For Those About to Rock (We Salute You)," and "Thunderstruck." As evidence of their international success, AC/DC played the 1991 Monsters of Rock festival in Moscow, Russia, for 1.6 million fans.

Plugged in, Angus Young spanks a variety of black and red Gibson SG Standards (with humbuckers and crown inlays) and backline of Marshall stacks—the very definition of economy. His late brother Malcolm preferred another basic axe, the Gretsch Jet Firebird G6131, fitted with a single bridge pickup, having simply removed the others. Angus's sole concession to guitar effects is use of *the preamp* of a Schaffer-Vega Diversity System to kick the front of his Marshalls for increased drive and volume. Other than that, the Young brothers created a sound that was all about simplicity—and that relentless AC/DC backbeat. ⚡

ANGUS AND MALCOLM MAINTAINED A RUTHLESS EFFICIENCY, NEVER OVERPLAYING.

Scott. Angus Young's forceful guitar solo is all about feel, with a combination of blues licks, fat vibrato, and double-stops inspired by his guitar hero, Chuck Berry. It bears noting that the genre of Australian "pub rock" also had a significant imprint on AC/DC; it's a genre that celebrates the

folded. Instead they hired frontman Brian Johnson and delivered their magnum opus, *Back in Black*, which sold over 25 million copies in the United States alone. With its ominous opener "Hells Bells," the music may have suggested the doom of Black Sabbath; but

BROTHERS IN ARMS, ANGUS AND MALCOLM YOUNG OF AC/DC.

⚡PAT TRAVERS

While the majority of '70s guitar heroes came out of the Eric Clapton/Jeff Beck/Jimmy Page school of heavy blues and proto-hard rock, there was a narrow slice of players deeply influenced by Jimi Hendrix's deep funk and psychedelia. Among them were Robin Trower, Eddie Hazel, Frank Marino, Uli Roth, Ernie Isley—and Canadian firecracker Pat Travers, who saw a Hendrix concert at the impressionable age of thirteen.

Describing that Jimi Hendrix show to Gary James at *Classicbands. com*, Travers (born April 12, 1954) remembered, "It was March 19, 1968 . . . I was in the 12th row, aisle seat of the Capital Theater in Ottawa, Canada, . . . a great theater . . . maybe about 2500 seats. It was an awesome place to see him. It was so overwhelming. . . . I just couldn't believe it. [Jimi] had three Marshall stacks. I had never seen one, let alone three! Noel Redding had three Sunn Coliseum bass stacks and it was so loud. [The concert] was so overwhelming to a 13-year-old kid."

Emerging mid-decade, Travers's early albums contained hard rock

sion turned the ensemble into a cutting-edge guitar crew. Peter "Mars" Cowling on bass and double-kick drummer Tommy Aldridge only elevated the fury of this quartet.

This sound manifested itself on their hyperkinetic *Live! Go for What You Know* album, spawning the single "(Boom Boom) Out Go the Lights." The crowd favorite cut took off at FM radio in 1979, blending a I-IV-V blues with hard rock, Van Halen–esque electricity, and a dash of Southern rock. Thrall's first solo demonstrated high-speed picking and tremolo-bar dives on a modified Stratocaster, while Travers, playing a Gibson Melody Maker modded with humbuckers, entered with flanged pentatonic runs before a thrilling double-guitar climax. Politically incorrect lyrics aside, it was a raucous concert stomper.

Another live track, "Stevie," found Pat Thrall executing cascade-echo effects over top of Travers's arpeggios, a stompbox trick attributed to Telecaster master Albert Lee. Using this technique, a guitarist plays a phrase of "dotted" quarter or eighth notes, and then

earning airplay with yet another updated blues, "Snortin' Whiskey" and its barrage of lead work and riffs. The combination of Travers's sweeping modulation tone and distortion, in tandem with Thrall's chorus pedal and whammy bar, sat at the forefront of guitar effects and tricks of that era. The album—the final effort of the Travers and Thrall collaboration—also contained covers of Cream's "Born under a Bad Sign" and a surprisingly sensitive take on Bob Markey's reggae jam "Is This Love?," graced with Thrall's deeply skilled rhythm work.

Of his own guitar style, Travers told the author in 1993, "A lot of modern metal players sound alike because they're playing licks that are derivative of material that's *already* derivative. They forget that the guitar can be a voice, not just a display of speed and technique. Hopefully, something like my version of [Cream's] 'Sittin' on Top of the World' will help bring that style of rock guitar back because I cut those leads completely live. Some of the notes in there are really honest." ⚡

"A LOT OF MODERN METAL PLAYERS . . . FORGET THAT THE GUITAR CAN BE A VOICE."

with a taste of funk—but the 1978 arrival of Van Halen energized his tone. He hired Pat Thrall (born August 26, 1953) as second guitarist in the new Pat Travers Band and the combination of Travers's blues-based Hendrixisms with Thrall's jagged fu-

uses a delay unit to *double* that phrase's speed with electronically created repeats. As Thrall showed in this power ballad, it's an impressive bit of guitar legerdemain.

In 1980 the Pat Travers Band followed up with the *Crash and Burn* LP,

While the rock and roll of Led Zeppelin drew from American and global music sources, groups like Deep Purple, Uriah Heep, Black Sabbath, and ELP created progressive and hard rock that was bluntly European and Middle Eastern in nature. Purple's resident guitar god Ritchie Blackmore had a gift for exotic modes, using harmonic and melodic minor, Phrygian, Byzantine, and Hungarian scales to create dark, sinister textures. A segment of rock fans lapped it up, and as a direct result, a host of new bands appeared, among them UFO, Scorpions, Whitesnake, Judas Priest, and Blackmore's post-Purp effort, Rainbow. These acts forged the Euro-metal movement that exploded in the 1980s.

A fresh generation of guitar masters also arrived, all proclaiming Blackmore as a modern-day Niccolò Paganini—the nineteenth-century violin virtuoso—but with a Stratocaster and 200-watt Marshalls. These young magicians, such as German axe-meisters Michael Schenker and Uli Jon Roth, added even more technical polish, from Hendrix-inspired whammy dives to Formula 1–speed picking.

Beginning in 1980, a shockwave of new U.K. bands hit, dubbed by the press NWOBHM—aka, the "New Wave of British Heavy Metal." This schism brought forth such institutions as Iron Maiden, Samson (with guitarist Paul Samson and future Maiden singer Bruce Dickinson), Motörhead, Saxon, Tygers of Pan Tang, and Def Leppard. Across the North Sea, the band Accept staked a claim for Germany, led by Flying V–wielding guitarist Wolf Hoffman. Sounding like the demonic offspring of Judas Priest and AC/DC, Accept's 1983 "Balls to the Wall" remains a definitive contribution to European metal.

Looking back, such modern subgenres of thrash, progressive, death, Scandinavian black, speed, and power metal can all be traced to these earlier European innovations. The music was sleek and fast, reveling in minor keys and instrumental virtuosity and containing lyrical allusions to demons, warfare, and Medieval sorcery.

Euro-metal was *Game of Thrones*—with electric guitars. ⚡

RITCHIE BLACKMORE [PART 2]

Not many rock musicians get a second chapter to their careers, but Ritchie Blackmore did. After leaving Deep Purple in 1975, Blackmore absorbed a minor New York band called Elf—led by unknown singer Ronnie James Dio—recorded a debut album, and then fired everyone but the talented frontman. Thus Ritchie Blackmore's Rainbow was born and became one of the groundbreaking acts of Euro-metal.

The band's sophomore album *Rainbow Rising* (1976) created real precedent, as Blackmore and Dio hybridized metal and prog-rock ambitions into something new and foreboding. "Tarot Woman" launched with a space-rock synthesizer intro, though the guitarist's vicious Stratocaster still dominated. The Middle Eastern–flavored "Stargazer" was an overt nod to Led Zeppelin's "Kashmir," clocking in over 8 minutes

to interfere with his quick picking—and glued-in the bolt-on necks for stability and to prevent string slippage. Other tone secrets included Velvet Hammer pickups, a passive MTC filter under the pots for greater tone control (built by his noted guitar tech, John "Dawk" Stillwell), and the preamp boost from an Aiwa reel-to-reel tape recorder.

His relationship to Stratocasters went back to a common source, as Blackmore told music journalist H. P. Newquist: "I was a big fan of Jimi Hendrix. His guitar didn't make a normal guitar sound; it used to come out and punch you in the face. I wondered how he did it, and thought, 'Must be the Fender; I want to try one of those things.' For one thing, the humbucking pickups I'd used [earlier] were far more forgiving than a Fender. The Fender pickup—if you played the right note, it would reward you by

is my idol. The guy gets notes from nowhere, you know? Sometimes he finds notes that I just do not have on my guitar. When 'Shapes of Things' came out, everybody went, 'Oh my God, who is that—and why is he playing this Indian stuff? It shouldn't be allowed.' It was just too good."

By the early 1980s, the rock icon was taking Rainbow in a more commercial direction, getting airplay with streamlined material like "Since You've Been Gone," "I Surrender," and blatantly Foreigner-styled "Stone Cold." After a successful Deep Purple reunion, he finally put Rainbow on hiatus in the 1990s, launching a semi-acoustic group called Blackmore's Night. Said Ritchie, "It's a Renaissance folk-rock band with my wife, Candace, and quite a change from Rainbow. When I play electric guitar, I have to have short fingernails on my right hand. Then, after a month off, I have to grow them back to play fingerstyle; sometimes I resort to the acrylics to make my fingernails stronger for fingerstyle playing."

BEYOND HENDRIX, INFLUENCES INCLUDE AMERICAN COUNTRY GUITARISTS.

with slide and proto-shred solos. The scorching leads within "A Light in the Black" and "Kill the King" (from 1978's *Long Live Rock 'n' Roll*) only confirmed Blackmore as the fastest gun in heavy metal.

For gear, the Rainbow guitarist began moving from maple fretboards to scalloped rosewood fingerboards on his Strats. Blackmore used the only neck and bridge single-coil pickups—the middle pickup was screwed as low as possible so as not

going, 'Well done.' You fluff a note, it goes, 'You f*cked up, and we're going to make it very obvious that you f*cked up.' I found I could never get a Gibson to rival that attack."

Beyond Hendrix, Blackmore's other influences include American country guitarists he'd seen on English television as a youth, as well as the blues players like Mick Taylor and Shuggie Otis. As Blackmore further told Newquist, there's someone even higher up the list: "Jeff Beck

Yet in 2016, Blackmore surprised everyone by assembling a brand-new Rainbow lineup—and hitting the road for one last tour. ⚡

MICHAEL SCHENKER

There aren't many European guitarists more lauded than Michael Schenker, despite a rocky career and long periods of inactivity. Yet just as an influence, you'll find dozens of top players who point to Schenker as a guitar colossus. Armed with a Gibson Flying V, *cocked* wah pedal, and 50-watt Marshall half-stack amp, the German virtuoso became the fastest, cleanest, and most melodic leadman to ever grace a heavy metal stage. For his perilous 22nd-fret string bends alone—up to the very highest E note—Schenker's legend is secure.

Schenker (born January 10, 1955) was a teen prodigy, first joining his brother Rudolf's band Scorpions and later, UFO. His five-year association with the latter produced albums of near-biblical importance in hard rock circles. While their early LPs

seriously melodic guitar solo. On the subsequent U.S. tour, however, the pressures of roadwork began to wear on the young guitarist and he disappeared—not for the first time—and returned to Germany. In January 1979, UFO released the live album *Strangers in the Night*, now considered one of the critical recordings in the Euro-metal canon. Schenker was in prime form, and his Flying V attack was so compelling that guitarists are copping those runs decades later. Of particular note was the eleven-minute guitar spectacular "Rock Bottom" and flamethrowers like "Too Hot to Handle" and "Mother Mary."

Ironically, by the time of its release, Schenker had already quit the band. One can safely speculate about what lofty heights UFO might have achieved had the guitarist stayed

left it in that position—the 'sweet spot.' It was sometimes a Vox or occasionally an old Dunlop pedal."

After aborted auditions for Aerosmith and Ozzy Osbourne, the guitarist reemerged with his own Michael Schenker Group (MSG), gaining airplay in 1981 with "On and On." But the twenty-six-year-old guitarist's career had already peaked; since then, his career has risen and fallen several times. Today Schenker is back in the saddle, a solo artist who performs regularly for his Flying V–obsessed fans and using a Dean Michael Schenker V solidbody.

Mulling his enormous guitar legacy, Schenker reflected, "I was influenced by the original rock players, like Clapton, Page, Beck, Johnny Winter, and Leslie West, but didn't copy their licks after age 17. After that, I developed my own style and knew exactly what I wanted, as far as tone, playing and writing. What I brought to the Scorpions, UFO, and MSG was *originality*, but also a lot of feel and strong sense of melody. Of course, the Scorpions developed into an original band all their own, especially with the writing between [singer] Klaus Meine and my brother Rudolf. He writes very much like me, but simpler—we are both very emotion-based composers and guitarists." ⚡

"I JUST PLUGGED THE FLYING V STRAIGHT INTO THE WAH AND AMP."

were anemically produced (by Ten Years After bassist Leo Lyons), UFO eventually found producer/engineer Ron Nevison and delivered an authoritative work in 1977, *Lights Out*. Schenker's blistering breaks on the title cut established him as a rising wizard, executing blues-scale runs, repeated licks, and minor modes at frightening tempos.

Released in 1978, *Obsession* confirmed UFO as one of the best acts out of England, balancing anthems with radio-ready material like "Only You Can Rock Me" and its

on—top-tier rock status seemed attainable—but the simple fact remained that the German was gone. UFO's fortunes dwindled accordingly.

Of his 1970s-era gear, Schenker told the author, "I just plugged the Flying V straight into the wah and amp, everything probably set on 10. It was one of those older, Plexiglas 50-watt Marshalls, but you needed to know what you wanted, sound-wise, in order to get a good tone. With the wah pedal, I used to just sweep through the range and stop when I found the sound I liked. Then I just

OF HIS 1970S-ERA GEAR, MICHAEL SCHENKER SAID, "I JUST PLUGGED THE FLYING V STRAIGHT INTO THE WAH AND AMP."

SCOTT GORHAM & BRIAN ROBERTSON

The most revered *guitar* band to emerge from Ireland, Thin Lizzy had a singular hard-rock attack, fronted by bassist Phil Lynott's smoky vocals and Celtic song imagery. Many gifted guitarists also passed through its ranks—including the iconic Gary Moore—but the ultimate pairing remains Brian Robertson and Scott Gorham, who drove the band in its mid-1970s heyday.

Aside from minor hits "Whiskey in the Jar" and "The Rocker" earlier in the decade (with original guitarist Eric Bell), Thin Lizzy didn't strike gold until 1976's *Jailbreak*. Its studio production wasn't stellar (Gorham told the author, "It sounded like it was recorded in a shoebox, in 1938"), but the LP contained anthems galore—obviously the sing-along hit "The Boys Are Back in Town"—but also "Cowboy Song," "Emerald," "Warriors," and "Jailbreak." Throughout

The years 1976–1979 proved the band's peak, as they torched studio platters like *Johnny the Fox*, *Bad Reputation*, and *Black Rose* (where Moore returned to replace Robertson). A fiery live act, Thin Lizzy's double-LP *Live & Dangerous* remains one of the gold standards of '70s concert albums.

To understand who played what on these albums, Gorham offered more melodic leads, displaying that Clapton soul and swirl of MXR Phase 90 phaser. Robertson—barely out of his teens—delivered fast, angular wah-wah licks. Robbo's most famous lead, however, can be heard in the live-album ballad "Still in Love with You," a crescendo of bends, sustained notes, and superfat tone. He said, "Peter Green was my first and biggest influence. I listened a lot to the early Thin Lizzy stuff as well, so I was heavily influenced by [orig-

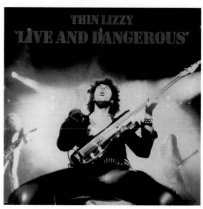

Of his famed "black beauty" Les Paul Custom, Robbo laughed: "That guitar was a piece of sh*t! I just picked it up because it looked great with my white jeans—but it played like a bitch and I sold it in L.A. on the *Bad Reputation* tour in 1977. For echo, I used an old WEM Copycat tape unit, something I wouldn't do today, but it worked out well for the purpose at the time. My wah was a Colorsound."

At their zenith, the quartet earned headliner status in the United Kingdom, Ireland, Canada, and Australia but only managed cult status in America, a factor some attribute to fans resisting a rock band with a black frontman. Yet coupled with Lynott's lyrics about Ireland, history, and tales of machismo, Lizzy carved their own niche—even more when "The Boys Are Back in Town" found new life at sporting events and in Hollywood (such as Pixar's *Toy Story* trailers). Today the song is a global pop phenomenon.

ONE OF THE MOST THRILLING LIVE ACTS IN METAL HISTORY.

its grooves, Scottish-born Robertson (aka *Robbo*, born February 12, 1956) and American-bred Gorham (born March 17, 1951) traded solos like hot potatoes and wove intricate harmonies like never before. When asked if the tandem guitars of the Allman Brothers Band were an influence, Gorham responded, "Actually, it was more of Wishbone Ash's approach to harmonies that shaped us, like on the *Argus* album. For my own guitar influence, I point to Eric Clapton, especially his natural *vib* [wrist vibrato]."

inal Lizzy guitarist] Eric Bell and the rough demos with Gary Moore, who was in the band before Scott and I joined in 1974."

For gear, the Robertson/Gorham team couldn't have rigs any more basic, each using Gibson Les Pauls and a phalanx of Marshall stacks. Gorham went with a cherry sunburst Deluxe with mini-humbuckers, shrugging, "I saw a Les Paul Standard in the store I *really* wanted—but the band just couldn't afford it at the time. So I ended up with the Deluxe."

For their blowout concerts alone, the Irish outfit will be remembered as one of the most thrilling live acts in metal history. As many headliners found out too late, Thin Lizzy was the *last* band you wanted as your opening act. ⚡

BRIAN ROBERTSON AND SCOTT GORHAM AND THEIR LES PAULS DROVE THIN LIZZY IN THE BAND'S MID-1970s HEYDAY.

GLENN TIPTON & K. K. DOWNING

If Black Sabbath is the symbolic godhead of metal, Judas Priest is its satanic offspring, a band that's 100 percent titanium to its core. Like Ozzy Osbourne, frontman Rob Halford is a figure who seems to define the genre, clad in studded leather and sitting astride a motorcycle—*on-stage*! Behind him, the twin-guitar fury of Glenn Tipton and K. K. Downing reinforced Priest's alchemy. Even their slow ballads are metal.

Both Tipton (born October 25, 1947) and Downing (born October 27, 1951) are from the 1960s/1970s school of guitar, learning licks from Eric Clapton, Jeff Beck, Jimmy Page, Jimi Hendrix, Ritchie Blackmore, and Peter Green. As Downing noted on *kkdowning.net*, "Hendrix was my idol. He was absolutely incredible and I don't think there'll ever be anyone else quite like

force and connected them with Tom Allom, the producer/engineer who would shape their sound for years to come. Once the 1980s arrived, so did the hits, as Judas Priest delivered "Breaking the Law," "Living after Midnight," "Heading Out to the Highway," and "Electric Eye" for the wide-eyed MTV generation. Suddenly, Judas Priest became one of the biggest concert draws in the world.

On guitar, Tipton and Downing were solid soloists, dropping distorted, skittering runs like bombs—but the *real* Judas Priest guitar lesson is about rhythm riffs and power chords. Unlike the trope of a "guitar hero" with mind-blowing chops and techniques, the Priest pair were all about locking into a groove with vicious barre chords. "Victim of Changes," from the live album, is a defining example,

Downing is a lifelong proponent of Flying V shapes, starting with Gibson models, but then moving into custom Vs built by Hamer, ESP, and KxK. Both guitarists also possessed numerous rack effects units, helping ignite the '80s fad of a "refrigerator" of rack gear, so named for their onstage resemblance to said kitchen appliance.

In the '90s and 2000s, the arrival of higher-gain amps made Priest sound even heavier and more menacing—their mid-career masterpiece "Judas Rising" is as dangerous a track as they ever recorded. Citing conflicts with management, Downing left the band in 2011 and was replaced with a fiery young shredder named Richie Faulkner; Tipton stepped down later that decade for health reasons.

TIPTON AND DOWNING DROPPED DISTORTED, SKITTERING RUNS LIKE BOMBS.

him." Tipton added on his own official website, ". . . as a guitar player, my main inspiration was Rory Gallagher. I saw him play in Taste many times and he really inspired me, not just musically, but also in the amount of energy and feel he put out."

With a few middling albums under its belt, Judas Priest finally delivered the all-metal goods on 1978 albums *Stained Class* and *Hell Bent for Leather*, followed by 1979's *Unleashed in the East*, a live album recorded in Japan. The concert LP positioned Priest as a rising

the guitarists supporting a thundering beat rather than show-off solos.

For gear, eardrum-piercing Marshall amplifiers were an obvious part of the story. For guitars, Tipton said on his website, "I have used numerous guitars over the years. These include SGs . . . and also [I] started using a modified CBS-era Fender Stratocaster with DiMarzio Super-Distortion pickups. For the *Screaming for Vengeance* tour, I added a chrome pickguard. . . . Around '84, I switched to a custom-made Hamer Phantom, plus my own distinctive Hamer GT."

Today Halford leads the quintet with newer members—plus original bassist Ian Hill—but the iconic Priest sound was forged in the 1970s–2000s. In the world of all things loud, there's really nothing as spectacular as a turbocharged Judas Priest riff, hell-bent for leather. ⚡

K. K. DOWNING AND GLENN TIPTON OF JUDAS PRIEST PERFORM AT NEW YORK'S NASSAU COLISEUM IN 1984.

RUDOLF SCHENKER, ULI JON ROTH & MATTHIAS JABS

You really can't get any more Euro-metal than Scorpions. A rock-and-roll institution from Germany, the quintet whipped up '70s power metal but became MTV darlings in the '80s with tight rockers and ballads. Their core was singer Klaus Meine and rhythm guitarist Rudolf Schenker, but also introduced lead guitarists Matthias Jabs, Uli Jon Roth, and Rudy's younger brother, Michael Schenker. To date Scorpions has sold over 100 million albums globally.

The group launched with the Schenker brothers on guitar, but Michael soon left for UFO; in came Roth (born December 18, 1954), a Strat-slinger who worshipped Jimi Hendrix. By 1976's masterful *Virgin Killer*, it was clear that Uli Roth was no ordinary player. Instead of rehashing old Eric Clapton and Jimmy Page blues scales, the Teutonic titan was conversant in advanced modes and harmonies, as well as possessing remarkable picking and a cocked-wah tone. He

solo, Roth told journalist Andy Craven for *Dinosaur Guitar Rock*, ". . . I did the train whistle on the guitar with the E♭7 chord . . . the runs were just simulating the general vibe of a train that has to be caught, [one] that's running away."

Even more terrifying was his playing on the 1978 live album *Tokyo Tapes*, containing "Speedy's Coming"—perhaps the ultimate balance of Rudolf's punky riffing and Roth's fret burning. Yet desiring to express-sive himself more personally, the lead guitarist left for a solo career. One of Roth's most interesting post-Scorpions innovations was to create custom six- and seven-string "Sky" guitars—each with *30 to 40 frets*—allowing him to play high solos notes only dogs can hear. These are one-of-a-kind solidbodies for a seriously unique guitar wizard.

Into his wake came Michael Schenker, who'd just quit UFO in time to appear on the *Lovedrive* album and play live dates. As heard

Jabs got down to work with simpli-fied, Michael Schenker–style leads on mega-hits like "No One Like You" and "Rock You Like a Hurricane," along with many power ballads. A solid guitarist, certainly, but the Matthias Jabs/Rudolf Schenker guitar era was less about guitar solos and more about *writing* hard rock for their millions of fans. In that, Scorpions has been tremendously successful.

For gear, Jabs is best known for his "striped" Gibson and Dommen-get Explorers, sometimes fitted with a locking-vibrato system, as well as the occasional Fender Stratocaster. Rudolf Schenker, like his brother, is closely associated with the Gibson Flying V, though he also plays custom Dommenget V axes.

In hindsight the Scorpions guitar saga can be broken up into two primary chapters: the guitar supremacy of the Uli Jon Roth epoch and the platinum Matthias Jabs years. Throughout it all Rudolf Schenker has held down the fort, putting the group's songs first—and supporting them with some of the most ferocious power chords of all time. Schenker is, without a doubt, Euro-metal's premier rhythm guitarist. ⚡

SOME OF THE MOST FEROCIOUS POWER CHORDS OF ALL TIME.

picked up where flashes like Deep Purple's Ritchie Blackmore and Focus's unsung Jan Akkerman left off, adding more aggression, dexterity, and blasts of pure Hendrix (listen to "Polar Nights").

With Rudolf providing a bed-rock of barre chords, Roth was free to rip on "Pictured Life" and the feedback-laden Mixolydian runs of "Catch Your Train." Of that latter

on the guitar-intensive instrumental "Coast to Coast," this would appear to be a heavenly combination of brotherly metal, but Michael followed Uli Roth out the door. Already in the wings, new guitarist Matthias Jabs was ready to go.

As it turned out, Jabs (born October 25, 1955) was the right man for a band on the verge of platinum fame. Without the ego of his predecessors,

TOP: ULI JON ROTH, POST-SCORPIONS IN 1985.
BOTTOM: RUDOLF SCHENKER AND MATTHIAS JABS WITH THE SCORPIONS AT ROSEMONT, ILLINOIS, 1984.

DAVE MURRAY & ADRIAN SMITH

There aren't many metal bands whose sound can be described as "swashbuckling," but that's the sonic signature of Iron Maiden. With tales of warfare, ancient history, and heroic valor, Maiden anthems evoke epic grandeur, thanks to Bruce Dickinson's soaring, near-operatic vocals and the power riffs of bassist and chief writer Steve Harris. Weave in the guitar army of Dave Murray, Adrian Smith and, much later, Janick Gers, and you have British hard rock that's justifiably earned a worldwide following.

The Maiden formula brings together the Euro thump of Black Sabbath, Deep Purple, UFO, and Thin Lizzy, stoking a sense of drama and theatricality. The Murray/Smith team deployed minor-key chord vamps draped with harmonized melodies in the Lizzy style. As Smith told the author, "As well as Purple and Free, you had Humble Pie, another of my favorite bands, and I used to see Michael Schenker in London when he played with UFO. Also, I liked Pat

in trade, heard in "Two Minutes to Midnight," "Powerslave," and "The Number of the Beast," with dizzying guitar leads and minor-chord chunks flying in every direction. Tracks like "Children of the Damned" start with chorused acoustic guitar and a minor-key ballad before building to a massive climax.

Of their writing and arranging style, Murray told Bret Adams in *Vintage Guitar Magazine*, "Even from [our] very first album, 'Phantom of the Opera' was 7 or 8 minutes long. . . . Songs like 'Rime of the Ancient Mariner' [and] 'Hallowed Be Thy Name' are [also] supposed to be that way. . . . You're creating something that's *building*. I think it's just part of the identity of Iron Maiden; a lot of our albums start with a slow, moody part then jump into an upbeat section. . . . It's all about the songs."

For gear, Murray and Smith favor a variety of Gibson Les Pauls and SGs—plus the inevitable wall of Marshall stacks. But the standard

[or] 20 years. It has Seymour Duncan pickups and a tortoiseshell scratch plate. I also use a couple of Les Pauls—one that has a Floyd Rose [whammy] and a Standard."

Smith also told the author, "I did play a Les Paul for many years, but the main reason I use a Jackson super-strat with humbuckers is because it blends better with the other guitarists. With three of us, sometimes the intonation can be a problem—when you've got three guitars playing the same chord in the same position, you're going to get a little sourness. Also spending two hours onstage, hauling a Les Paul around is not that much fun, while Strats are so much more comfortable to play. On my signature Jackson, I have a humbucker and two single coils, and use the neck pickup single coil for really authentic Strat sounds on a couple of songs. But overall, it just seems to work with the other Maiden guys, all of us using strat-type guitars."

THE MAIDEN FORMULA BRINGS TOGETHER THE EURO THUMP, STOKING A SENSE OF DRAMA.

Travers and the guys in Thin Lizzy: Scott Gorham, Brian Robertson, and, of course, Gary Moore. Thin Lizzy was a massive influence on a lot of British kids in the '70s."

With their 1980 debut, Iron Maiden amassed a rabid core of fans during the so-called New Wave of British Heavy Metal. Maiden's long-form compositions proved their stock

Maiden axe is a Stratocaster, or other strat-style guitar, fitted with humbucker pickups. This offers the advantage of a fast, double-cutaway neck and dive-bombing tremolo bar, with the additional low-noise operation of a humbucker. Murray further noted to *Vintage Guitar Magazine*, "[My main guitar is a] California Series Strat I've been using for . . . 15

IRON MAIDEN'S ADRIAN SMITH (LEFT) AND DAVE MURRAY (RIGHT) WITH "NEW GUY" JANICK GERS.

RANDY RHOADS

It's no small irony that one of Euro-metal's best guitarists was—an American. Yet no question, the two metal masterpieces Randy Rhoads recorded with Ozzy Osbourne—*Blizzard of Ozz* and *Diary of a Madman*—are squarely in that European camp, with dark chord progressions, harmonic-minor chills, and plenty of continental *Sturm und Drang*. The tragedy, of course, is that fans lost Rhoads after the briefest of careers, barely lasting two years. Yet over forty years later, guitarists all over the planet are still talking about this lost hero and those ferocious solos of his.

Rhoads's playing spoke to a knowledge of Ritchie Blackmore and Michael Schenker riffs, plus ample doses of Jimmy Page, Jeff Beck, and his old L.A. rival, Eddie Van Halen. Discussing Rhoads's guitar influences with his friend Kelly Garni, the original bassist in Quiet Riot, he said, "A big influence on [him] . . . was Alice Cooper's guitarist, Glenn Buxton."

Blizzard of Ozz was released in the United States in early 1981 and shot up the charts, instantly saving Ozzy's music career. The album kicked off with "I Don't Know," a cooker that sounds like Black Sabbath on steroids. Its solo is pure Rhoads, a frantic mass of bends, jittery wrist vibrato, and muted arpeggios. The radio favorite "Crazy Train" was a blend of Euro riffery with sunny SoCal rock, while its multitracked solo launched with baroque two-handed tapping—a straight evolution from Van Halen's "Eruption." Said guitar star Steve Vai in the rock-doc *Ozzy Osbourne: Thirty Years after the Blizzard*, "I remember when I first heard 'Crazy Train' and then its freight-train of a guitar came screaming in. I think it's the first rock track I heard where the solo came in—and I got scared."

Rhoads's guitar rig also helped set the standard for modern metal, and he's identified with several

guitars, among them, a white Gibson Les Paul Custom. Another key axe was the Sandoval Dot V built by luthier Karl Sandoval in the summer of 1979, just prior to landing the Ozzy gig. A polka-dot solidbody with "bowtie" inlays (one of Rhoads's stage trademarks in the Quiet Riot years), the solidbody had a vibrato bridge, DiMarzio humbuckers, and neck taken from an old Danelectro. Rhoads paid $738 for the instrument.

Also in Rhoads's arsenal were a pair of offset V-style guitars designed by Grover Jackson, Tim Wilson, and Mike Shannon. One black, one white, these Jacksons had Seymour Duncan humbuckers, vibrato bridges, and set-neck designs. The now-iconic design—designated the Jackson Rhoads model—became a quintessential metal axe after Rhoads's death, and the list of metal-men who've used them is impressive, including Megadeth's Dave Mustaine, Metallica's Kirk Hammett, and Children of Bodom's Alexi Laiho.

On March 19, 1982, the twenty-five-year-old guitarist died in a freak airplane accident, a tour prank gone horribly awry. For a player who had such a short career, though, Rhoads remains a beloved guitar innovator. Along with Van Halen, you can hear Rhoads's playing as the bridge between the Euro-metal of the 1970s and heavy MTV bands of the 1980s, notably Dokken, Dio, Ratt, and Whitesnake (not to mention his Ozzy successors, Jake E. Lee and Zakk Wylde). Today Rhoads's riffs are beyond being merely *influential*—they're fundamental lessons for every metal guitarist. ⚡

FOR A PLAYER WHO HAD SUCH A SHORT CAREER, RHOADS REMAINS A BELOVED INNOVATOR.

Randy liked all the weird noises and feedback that Buxton came up with. . . . Then Mick Ronson came along with Bowie, and he [liked those noises, too] . . . when later, I heard Randy's big guitar solo on the live Ozzy *Tribute* record, I [laughed] because there were all these licks . . . he [played] when we were [teenagers]."

RANDY RHOADS'S RIG HELPED SET THE STANDARD FOR MODERN METAL, AND HE'S OFTEN IDENTIFIED WITH A WHITE GIBSON LES PAUL CUSTOM.

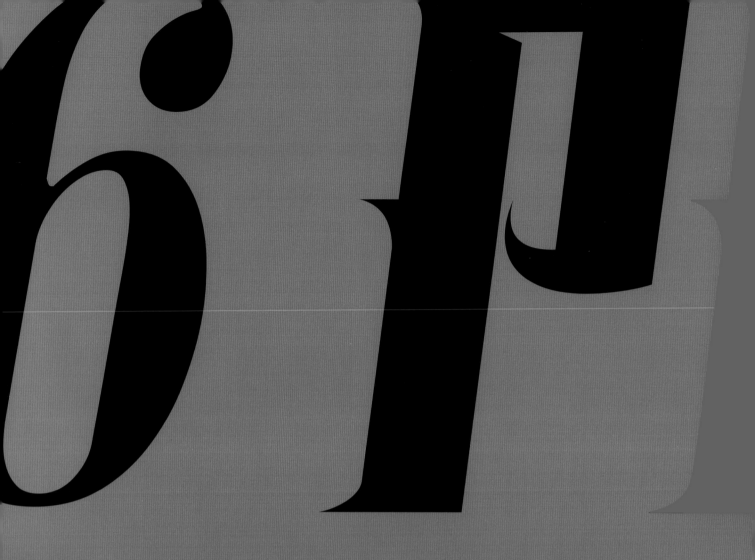

Bubbling up from psychedelia, British Invasion, soul, and 1960s folk revival, the style we now call progressive rock—or *prog* for short—was initially just rock with lofty ambitions. Some of the early acts vaguely deemed "progressive" were the Jimi Hendrix Experience, Jefferson Airplane, Fairport Convention, Soft Machine, and Traffic. But gradually the genre began integrating symphonic-classical sounds, jazz harmony, and extended compositions; British ensembles like Yes, Emerson, Lake & Palmer, and Genesis soon became emblematic of this high-brow FM offshoot.

Just as quickly another mutation emerged, bringing hard rock into the artsy mix. Early examples are Mountain's "Theme for an Imaginary Western" and "Nantucket Sleighride," with Leslie West's distortion riffs over dramatic Hammond organ. Jethro Tull's breakout *Aqualung* album found lyrical acoustic guitar countered by Les Paul thud. King Crimson's Robert Fripp was experimenting with metallic flavors as early as 1973's "Lark's Tongue in Aspic (Parts 1 & 2)." Deep Purple and Rainbow fused metal and classical concepts, almost weekly.

The proverbial elephant in the room, jazz-rock fusion exploded onto the scene. The Mahavishnu Orchestra released two wildly influential albums—*Inner Mounting Flame* (1971) and *Birds of Fire* (1973)—each superimposing the mach-speed guitar of John McLaughlin over Black

FULL POWER

Sabbath–like volume levels. Fast on its heels came Billy Cobham's *Stratus* album (with future Deep Purple axeman Tommy Bolin); Return to Forever; and Jeff Beck, who slapped heavy riffage into *Blow by Blow* and *Wired*. These were heady times for loud guitar players.

From this explosion came what today's listeners recognize as prog-metal, the genre achieving corporeal form with Rush and Kansas, and evolving through Queensrÿche, Dream Theater, and Fate's Warning. Today prog-metal can be found on every continent. Case in point: a self-styled "classical metal" act from India called Sitar Metal, featuring a sitarist who taps and blazes like a guitar shredder.

Metal and prog were simply made to go together. ⚡

KERRY LIVGREN & RICH WILLIAMS

Progressive rock largely emanated from Great Britain, continental Europe, and Canada—with one *ginormous* exception.

Hailing from the midwestern U.S. city of Topeka, the band Kansas tore up the charts in the spring of 1977 with a stomper called "Carry on Wayward Son," making them FM sensations and earning headline gigs at Madison Square Garden. Their spin on prog-rock was to dose it with molten guitar in the manner of Cream and Mountain yet sprinkle in baroque violin and electronic keyboards. The formula worked—and Kansas became dominant in both hard rock and progressive categories for several years.

Despite the proggy pretensions, guitarists Kerry Livgren (born September 18, 1949) and Rich Williams (born February 1, 1950) were, in many ways, conventional '70s players, coming from the Clapton/Beck/Page canon of Marshall tone and blues-scale runs. But therein lies the magic, as Kansas crossed high-gain

in the Wind," became a massive, million-selling single in 1978. Ironically Livgren originally devised its fingerstyle chord part as a simple guitar exercise. On vinyl the greatest Kansas epoch lasted from 1974–1979, including multiplatinum albums *Leftoverture* and *Point of Know Return*. However, definitive Livgren/Williams guitar could be heard well before then on early epics like "Song for America" and "Mysteries and Mayhem."

Kansas also had a renowned work ethic, putting in hours of deep rehearsal to synchronize the music's complicated parts. As Williams told Bret Adams in *Vintage Guitar Magazine*, "In our early days, we were doing an interview and they asked Kerry, 'Who's your biggest influence?' He said, 'Probably Rich, because we play together all the time.' We were working on equipment together . . . [on] guitars and guitar tone and different things. You're not in competition, but constantly working together."

The pair's six-string relationship was so intertwined that listen-

really wasn't my strength. There's a tremendous irony that had to do with that. When I wrote 'Dust in the Wind,' which was by far Kansas' biggest hit, it was an acoustic song. . . . We went into the studio and I was the one who played the acoustic. I had to borrow Rich's Martin D-28 to play that. And so, here I am, almost exclusively an electric guitarist and the most famous work I ever did was on an acoustic."

For gear, Williams and Livgren were primarily Gibson men in the 1970s. Les Pauls were a central part of their arsenals, but also ES-335 semi-hollowbodies and, for Livgren, the occasional SG, Strat, and Dean Z. For Williams, he sometimes grabbed a blonde Gibson L6-S, an oddball from Gibson's ill-fated Norlin era. Amps were 100-watt Marshall heads fed into single 4 x 12 slant cabinets; external effects were almost nonexistent for these tone purists. After Livgren left the band in the 1980s, Williams converted to Paul Reed Smith solidbodies, such as the PRS Custom 24, and has been playing them ever since. Today Kansas is still touring and recording for their fiercely loyal fans around the planet. ⚡

LISTENERS COULDN'T TELL WHERE ONE PLAYER STARTED AND THE OTHER LEFT OFF.

guitars with airy Bach figures and soaring lead vocals from singer/organist Steve Walsh. "Wayward Son" became a hit because of the avalanche of hooks it contained—every guitar figure, organ lick, and vocal was a "hook" that grabbed the listener and made the song unforgettable.

Their follow-up hit, the spartan acoustic-guitar ballad "Dust

ers couldn't tell where one player started and the other left off. Of the eternal "*Who played what*?" question, Livgren told Brian D. Holland of *Guitar International*, "It was a bit interchangeable. But the majority of the time I did the lead work and Rich did the supportive role. However, Rich probably did 80 or 90 percent of the acoustic work, which

KERRY LIVGREN (TOP) AND RICH WILLIAMS OF KANSAS PERFORM WITH THE BAND IN MIAMI, FLORIDA, 1977.

⚡ ALEX LIFESON

In a celebrated career with Rush, guitarist Alex Lifeson evolved from a Jimmy Page–loving riffer into a daring explorer of progressive and post-punk sounds—ultimately developing his own singular voice. For over forty years, Rush recorded and toured heavily, the axeman grabbing a dizzying array of six-string models to ply his trade.

Hailing from Toronto, Rush couldn't hide their Brit-metal aspirations on a strong 1974 debut—butt-kicking tracks like "Working Man" and "What You're Doing" were straight from the *Led Zeppelin II* playbook. Nearly dropped from their label two years later, the trio made a Hail Mary pass with the *2112* album and, surprisingly, scored gold via the twenty-minute title cut. "2112" was also a tour de force of Lifeson guitar fury, with glimpses of acoustic guitar—one of the young Canadian's emerging talents.

The 1976 live LP *All the World's a Stage* concluded Rush's hard-rock chapter. It was also a display of Marshall-fueled overdrive, wah-wah, and Maestro Echoplex, as heard on "By-Tor and the Snow Dog"—a sign of thickly applied guitar effects to

The trio followed with two entirely progressive albums, *A Farewell to Kings* (1977) and *Hemispheres* (1978), with Lifeson exploring dynamic nuances reminiscent of Steve Howe of Yes and Steve Hackett of Genesis yet not losing that relentless Rush assault. There were examples of his nylon-string classical abilities during the intros to "A Farewell to Kings" and "The Trees." A complex suite, "La Via Strangiato" revealed the blinding instrumental skills of Lifeson, bassist Geddy Lee, and drummer Neil Peart; conversely, one of the guitarist's slower breaks here pointed toward the U.K. blues of Peter Green and David Gilmour. By then, he'd also gravitated to Gibson semi-hollowbodies, including the ES-335, tobacco 'burst ES-345, and the 1976 ES-355TD called "Whitey." Lifeson also grabbed a Gibson ES-1275 doubleneck to play 12-string parts in concert—dramatically matched onstage by Lee's black Rickenbacker doubleneck.

With audiences rapidly growing, Rush rose to headliner status on U.S. arena tours; and the 1980 album *Permanent Waves* proved their break-

Holdsworth and Eddie Van Halen. A prime example is "Limelight," with its delicate arpeggios and soaring whammy and echo drones, again revealing that Steve Hackett influence. He also made fresh gear choices, including a Gibson Howard Roberts Fusion semi-hollowbody and round-back Ovation acoustic-electrics for stage work.

Later in the 1980s, Lifeson moved to PRS solidbodies, saying, "PRS makes the best guitars I've ever played; they really come out of the case perfect. They have a new model that has sort of a Les Paul feel—but with a shorter scale neck that's a little fatter, too." After the millennium, the Rush man returned to his first love, the Les Paul, helping develop the Alex Lifeson Axcess model with a locking Floyd vibrato and smooth neck-heel, to grab and bend those screaming high notes.

Despite the hoopla for his lead-guitar work, Lifeson is a consummate rhythm player, much like his teen hero, Pete Townshend of The Who. If you consider that a typical Rush concert consisted of hundreds, if not *thousands*, of individual riffs, fiery chord progressions, and arpeggios, Lifeson used his deep musical memory not only to recall each one but to execute them with precision. Onstage with Canada's greatest rock band, his playing was, in a word, flawless. ⚡

AFTER THE MILLENNIUM, LIFESON RETURNED TO HIS FIRST LOVE, THE LES PAUL.

come. As Lifeson (born August 27, 1953) told the author of his smokin' Gibson, seen all over the LP's gatefold, "The Les Paul I used on the live album was a 1970 tobacco-sunburst Standard. In fact, that guitar was on *all* the early Rush records."

out, thanks to the gently pandering single "The Spirit of Radio." In 1981 Lifeson read the tea leaves of guitar fashion and jumped to a modded white strat-style with a humbucker (the Hentor Sportscaster), inspired by trendsetting fretburners like Allan

ALEX LIFESON WITH RUSH IN 2008. DESPITE ATTENTION FOR HIS LEAD WORK, LIFESON IS A CONSUMMATE RHYTHM PLAYER.

MICHAEL WILTON & CHRIS DEGARMO

One of the chief architects of progressive metal, Queensrÿche rose steadily through the 1980s and exploded in 1990 to become, briefly, a major American band. Their essential formula was to graft the expansive hard rock of Rush with the cynical lyric approach of Pink Floyd's Roger Waters, forging a dystopian sound for the Reagan/Bush/Clinton era. They hit platinum with *Operation: Mindcrime* (1988), *Empire* (1990), and *Promised Land* (1994) along the way, earning a mass following and selling over 20 million albums. Their mega-selling power ballad "Silent Lucidity" was also nominated in several Grammy categories and won a pile of MTV Music Awards.

As players, original guitarists Michael Wilton and Chris DeGarmo proved themselves intelligent soloists who, like Rush's Alex Lifeson, crafted their solos into concise, eloquent

For instruments, the Queensrÿche axemen were devoted users of ESP solidbodies, known for super-strats built to exacting standards for metal guitarists and bassists. As Wilton told the author, "For live stuff, I use a few ESP models and a Les Paul Standard. The ESPs are three-pickup jobs with a five-way selector and a single/single/humbucker setup of Seymour Duncan pickups. They have a lot of tonal variety in them, plus ESP has been really good about building us guitars with whatever sound we're looking for for—whether they have different woods or pickups. Chris and I usually ask them to locate quality ash, mahogany, or maple tonewoods; but with all the resources drying up, it's getting hard to find good, aged wood."

Anyone familiar with Queensrÿche's work knows they frequently mixed acoustic and electric guitar

for better options of going direct. We use a lot of acoustics live, especially since 'Silent Lucidity.' We got it sounding good in those big arenas, but it can be tricky. There's a threshold where you can't turn the volume up anymore or you'll get feedback from the cavity of the guitar."

Recording their 1994 album *Promised Land* at a remote house in Washington's San Juan Islands, Queensrÿche went to extraordinary lengths to cut their electric and acoustic guitars in less-than-ideal conditions. Remembers DeGarmo, "The acoustic for 'Out of Mind' was taped in the living room of this neurosurgeon's retreat overlooking the Puget Sound. 'Bridge' was recorded in their bathroom; sometimes, we had to unplug the refrigerator to make it quiet enough. In fact, we had to entirely revamp the power going into the place because the house was really wired to make Pop Tarts in a toaster—not power a bunch of loud guitar amps." ⚡

WILTON AND DEGARMO CRAFTED THEIR SOLOS INTO CONCISE STATEMENTS.

statements rather than blowing notes all over the place. Of note on *Empire* were such multifaceted rockers as "Best I Can" and "Jet City Woman," which benefited as much from Wilton and DeGarmo's tight ensemble playing as high-voltage but melodic leads. (Another Rush connection: Peter Collins produced both *Empire* and several albums by the Canadian power trio.)

in one song, much as Led Zeppelin, Yes, Jethro Tull, and ELP did decades earlier. Not surprisingly, both DeGarmo and Wilton took their acoustic instruments quite seriously, especially in the perilous area of amplifying them for live performance. Said DeGarmo, "I have some old Martins and Taylors that I really like; onstage, we're always looking

---

QUEENSRÿCHE GUITARISTS MICHAEL WILTON AND CHRIS DEGARMO CRAFTED THEIR SOLOS INTO CONCISE, ELOQUENT STATEMENTS.

JOHN PETRUCCI

While Queensrÿche quickly rose to become a chart-topping band, Dream Theater took the slow road. They perfected a style of intense virtuoso metal, recorded, and toured year in and year out. The gradual result was a loyal fanbase around the world, many of whom came to shows just to witness Dream Theater's resident six-string wizard, John Petrucci. The Long Island guitarist grew up listening to skillful fusion and metal guitarists, notably influenced, he once said, "*by all the Als and all the Steves*," referring to Allan Holdsworth, Alex Lifeson, Al Di Meola, Steve Morse, Steve Howe, and Steve Vai, among others. From this, Petrucci wove a complex, technique-heavy style that is widely imitated throughout the metalverse.

Dream Theater came together at Boston's Berklee College of Music, where Petrucci, bassist John Myung, and drummer Mike Portnoy met as young students. After a few years, the quintet cut their breakthrough, *Images and Words*. Their 1991 single "Pull Me Under" perfectly captured the Dream

On the road, Dream Theater performs dizzying, mathematical, speed-freaked material onstage, with nary a bum note. Regarding his approach to memorizing the complex music, Petrucci told Tom Quayle of *Guitar Interactive Magazine*, "Everybody has their own [method]. Jordan [Rudess, Dream Theater's keyboardist] is a reader, so he has everything transcribed. . . . My short-term memory's really good. When we're in the studio . . . constructing a song . . . doing [it] piece by piece, I'm the only guy who can play it all the way through. But . . . my long-term memory is horrible, so when [we] go to prep for a tour, it's hell. I have to go back and learn the songs. . . . It takes me a while to get that, but once it's in, then I just practice the difficult parts over and over."

The guitarist is notoriously particular about guitar equipment. Originally an Ibanez endorser, Petrucci later created signature solidbodies with the Ernie Ball Music Man company, called the JP and Majesty se-

well as acoustic-piezo sounds. He said of the Majesty Purple Nebula model, "[It's] a neck-through design. [The neck's] center piece is maple and the two outside pieces are Honduran mahogany. . . . [It has] a quilted maple top. It has my signature DiMarzio pickups, the Dreamcatcher and the Rainmaker. There's an up to 20 dB boost on the Volume control [and] a coil-tap on the Tone control, [along with a] piezo system."

The core of his tone engine remains Mesa/Boogie tube amps, plus a Dunlop wah, other pedals, and a raft of digital effects. Petrucci was part of the first generation of metalers to have embraced MIDI rigs, using programmed MIDI controllers to determine every aspect of his guitar's signal path, as well as how the effects are deployed onstage.

Aside from Dream Theater, Petrucci is a sometime member of the instrumental metal quartet Liquid Tension Experiment and has toured with his heroes Joe Satriani and Steve Vai in the guitar-only G3 tours. He even married a metal riffer—wife Rena Sands played in the thrash band Meanstreak—and the husband-and-wife rockers still do guitar clinics together. Ironically two members of that all-woman metal band married two *other* members of Dream Theater! ⚡

THE CORE OF HIS TONE REMAINS MESA/BOOGIE TUBE AMPS, A DUNLOP WAH, AND A RAFT OF DIGITAL EFFECTS.

Theater assault, an explosion of Metallica and Rush mixed with the lofty crescendos of Yes and Genesis—and a supremely fretburning solo to top. The twenty-four-year-old guitarist was, almost overnight, one of the most-admired shredders alive.

ries. (*Trivia:* In its early days, Dream Theater was named Majesty.) These six-, seven-, and eight-string models are optimized for live performance, offering the guitar ace a vast range of tone options, from heavy humbucker doom to single-coil chime, as

THE

HEADBAN

BLK

The year 1980 was a watershed moment for heavy metal, fueled by major releases from AC/DC (*Back in Black*), Ozzy Osbourne (*Blizzard of Ozz*), Black Sabbath (*Heaven and Hell*), and Judas Priest (*British Steel*)—and setting the stage for a decade of headbanging. On August 1, 1981, there was another tremor, as a cable television channel called MTV broadcast its first video. From then on, '80s rock was an all-night party of music videos, giant festivals (such as the US Festival, LiveAid, and Rock in Rio), and albums that sold into the mega-millions.

While synth-pop and dance music were cloyingly prevalent, MTV also championed the metallic riffs of Twisted Sister's "We're Not Gonna Take It" and Quiet Riot's "Cum on Feel the Noize." Michael Jackson's crossover hit "Beat It" had a shreddy solo from Eddie Van Halen (over molten chords from Toto's Steve Lukather). Steve Stevens's ferocious, proto-shred solo on the Billy Idol hit "Rebel Yell" took hard rock into the future with drum machines and ray-gun effects. The glossy sounds of hair metal struck gold via Cinderella, Slaughter, Skid Row, and Poison.

There were other music machinations, most of it driven by financial strategies. Concert tours became product-driven events with corporate sponsors, logos, and heavy merchandising. For the first half of the decade, the cassette tape reigned; but by decade's end, the compact disc—the ubiquitous CD—became the audio format of choice and sales rocketed. While the film *This Is Spinal Tap* offered a savage parody of the industry, audiences adored it, especially fictional metal hero Nigel Tufnel, who cranked his Marshall amps "up to 11." Even niche magazines took off, as *Guitar for the Practicing Musician*, *Guitar Player*, *Musician*, and *Vintage Guitar Magazine* offered exclusive interviews, gear reviews, instructional lessons, and sheet music.

No question, the 1980s were a good time to be a hungry young metalhead. ⚡

PHIL COLLEN & STEVE CLARK

Def Leppard pulled off the ultimate magic trick: creating melodic, radio-friendly material that was *unquestionably* heavy metal. Part of the secret formula was employing producer Robert "Mutt" Lange and engineer Mike Shipley, who imbued their biggest records with audio rivaling the sonics of Queen and Boston. On guitar, Steve Clark (1960–1991) played on Def Lep's multiplatinum smashes *Pyromania* and *Hysteria*, along with lead flash Phil Collen (born December 8, 1957).

After two early albums associated with the New Wave of British Heavy Metal movement, original guitarist Pete Willis was let go during the *Pyromania* sessions. Phil Collen, imported from a band called Girl, filled the void and immediately upped Def Leppard's six-string game. "Stagefright" combines a verse of minor-key power chords with

the string gauge because I was using like .09s or something, and he had .010s on that Les Paul. I play .013s now but that's what started it off, with that Les Paul and Gary Moore."

The *Pyromania* singles "Photograph" and "Foolin'" helped sell the polished Def Leppard sound to radio, thanks to layers of overdubbed vocals with silky reverb—it became the band's audio trademark. Particularly on the mega-hit "Photograph," Collen's melodic lead work was ahead of the curve, and that quick shred lick at the end arrived well before anyone had heard of Yngwie, Satch, or Vai.

With big expectations, Def Leppard labored four years to craft a follow-up, at a whopping production price of $4.5 million. The resulting *Hysteria* album of 1987 is one of the defining 1980s hard-rock albums, every note buffed to perfection for airplay and videos. The band still relied

video, a rare Gibson XR-1, a precursor to the stripped-down Les Paul Studio series. Clark died from the effects of substance abuse in 1991 and was replaced by Vivian Campbell of Dio and Whitesnake fame. The six-string team of Collen and Campbell still hold down Def Leppard's guitar fort to this day.

During his early years with Def Leppard, Collen's main axe was a 1980 Ibanez Destroyer DT555. Its shape was basically a modified Gibson Explorer, with three uncovered white humbuckers laid against a black finish—a metal fashion statement for that era. Today Collen endorses a full range of Jackson USA Signature Phil Collen PC1 solidbodies, all super-strats with the Floyd Rose locking tremolo system, and a pickup configuration of a humbucker in the bridge, middle single-coil, and a sustainer pickup in the neck slot. In concert, the band also tunes their guitars and basses down to E♭, which assists the band members in singing the seemingly unreachable high notes that made Def Leppard famous. ⚡

MELODIC LEAD WORK AHEAD OF THE CURVE

a major-key chorus—*and* a speedy guitar solo from Collen, prophesying the shred boom.

For guitar influences, Phil Collen once met his Thin Lizzy hero Gary Moore, telling Nick Bowcott of Sweetwater, "I got to jam with [Moore] because he opened up for us on the *Pyromania* tour. I went in the dressing room; he had the [1959] Peter Green Les Paul. I'm like, 'Wow! That's Greeny . . .' [and] he said, 'Yeah, play it!' So we sat down . . . and played for like an hour. That was the start of me going heavier with

on mountains of reverb, notably their trademark vocals, but pushed the bass and drums to maximum levels. Instead of Marshall stacks, Collen and Clark heavily overdubbed with tiny Rockman headphone amps (invented by Boston guitarist Tom Scholz). Nearly every track from side 1 ended up on radio, from the pop rock of "Animal" to the bubblegum metal of "Pour Some Sugar on Me" and slicker L.A. glam of "Armageddon It."

For gear, Clark was known for rocking various Les Pauls, a Gibson doubleneck, and in the "Photograph"

STEVE CLARK AND PHIL COLLEN OF DEF LEPPARD PERFORM AT THE SAN REMO MUSIC FESTIVAL IN FEBRUARY 1988.

GARY MOORE

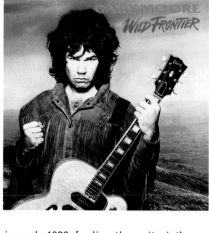

By 1980 Gary Moore was an established metal hero in the United Kingdom and Ireland—but something of a mythological figure in America, where he rarely toured. For his proto-shred work on Thin Lizzy's *Black Rose* album, some U.S. fans already knew what a fretboard demon he was, though commercial success proved elusive. After committing to a solo career, Moore spent the rest of the '80s exploring the depths of fiery hard rock and metal.

Moore's 1982 set *Corridors of Power* was a defiant statement, the opener "Don't Take Me for a Loser" using a Deep Purple-esque riff and Jeff Beck–evoking fusion solo. Long before anyone had heard of Yngwie Malmsteen, "End of the World" revealed his freakish picking speed with descending hammer-ons, bathed in unadulterated Stratocaster-through-Marshall tone. *Victims of*

psychedelia, and early hard-rock players, with particularly strong impressions from Eric Clapton, Jimi Hendrix, and Free's Paul Kossoff. But his top inspiration came from a beloved British bluesman, as Moore told the author: "My fat tone and emotional approach are a tribute to Peter Green. I remember when Green replaced Eric Clapton in John Mayall's Bluesbreakers and I later saw them play at Club Rado in Belfast. They opened with 'All Your Love' and I remember the floor shaking like mad. I'd never heard a Les Paul sound like that. Peter was using an old, rented amplifier which most people couldn't get a decent sound out of—but he still got the most amazing tone and bass end."

For his next solo album, 1985's *Run for Cover*, the Belfast guitarist developed a more contemporary sound, utilizing high-tech synthesiz-

in early 1986, fueling the guitarist's poignant follow-up, *Wild Frontier*, rife with Irish themes and savage metal riffs. It was arguably the finest solo album of his career, highlighted by the Celtic-themed "Over the Hills and Far Away" and virtuoso lead work on the title cut.

In 1990 Moore released *Still Got the Blues*, reinventing himself as a blues-rock artist. Thanks to the hit title ballad, the LP went gold in the United States; and, at last, Moore found the global recognition he'd been seeking. For gear, he also went back to the 1959 Les Paul 'burst he'd owned for decades. Here Moore recalls how he got his hands on that flametop—easily one of the most famous Gibsons of all time.

"After that Bluesbreakers show in Belfast, I thought, 'God, one day I would love to have a Les Paul like that—now I actually *own* the guitar Peter Green was playing that night. My band Skid Row once opened for Fleetwood Mac in Dublin, and he liked my playing so much he helped get us a deal and brought us to England. So you could say Peter discovered me. I got to know him and he lent me his '59 Les Paul for a while, eventually just about giving it to me for nothing. I've got a lot to thank him for. To me he's still the greatest blues guitarist ever." ⚡

MOORE SOAKED UP IDEAS FROM 1960s BLUES, PSYCHEDELIA, AND HARD-ROCK PLAYERS.

the Future (1983) served to reinforce Moore's metal mood, though "Empty Rooms" revealed another Gary Moore trademark: the poignant power ballad. With soul-wrenching guitar leads, these bittersweet, European-style ballads would remain part of his repertoire until a fatal heart attack in 2011 at age 58.

For influences, Moore (1952–2011) soaked up ideas from 1960s blues,

ers and sequencers, plus improved guitar sonics (the title cut bore similar production hallmarks to Billy Idol's "Rebel Yell"). By this time, Moore put down the Strat in favor of a Hamer Special solidbody; Gary Moore also reunited with Thin Lizzy singer Phil Lynott for the duet "Out in the Fields," where Moore dropped a high-velocity shred demonstration for the ages. Lynott died suddenly

GARY MOORE TEARS IT UP WITH HIS FIESTA RED-FINISHED STRATOCASTER.

JOAN JETT & LITA FORD

At one time, the sight of women playing electric guitars was rare, but 1970s artists like Bonnie Raitt and Heart began defying these once-intractable perceptions. An all-woman band called The Runaways joined the movement with its '76 debut album, adding a sound that mixed hard rock, glam, and proto punk. They didn't land any hits but received extensive coverage from the rock press and launched the careers of two genuine rock stars: Joan Jett and Lita Ford.

Rhythm guitarist Jett—heavily inspired by '70s glam bassist Suzi Quatro—scored a number of FM hits early in the decade, including the #1 blockbuster from 1981, "I Love Rock 'n Roll." Originally released by a British band, The Arrows, the Jett version was perfectly designed for the New Wave era, using blunt power chords and a catchy lyric to hook millions of listeners. There were no fast

who added its first humbucker). Discussing her later signature Gibson Melody Maker, Jett told writer Nick Cracknell of *MusicRadar*, "It's perfect for gigs as well as recording. For those of you performing live, you may understand the value of being able to shave off those split seconds between playing and interacting with the audience, especially if you use your hands to communicate. I can move between the killswitch, which mutes the guitar, and playing, and then back again without a lot of in-between motion."

Compared to her former bandmate, lead guitarist Lita Ford steered her post-Runaways career in a decidedly heavier direction, becoming a noted figure of glam metal—also known as hair metal for its absurdly puffed-up hairdos. She learned to play guitar in the classic metal era, telling Paul Rigg of Guitars Ex-

smash via a duet with Ozzy Osbourne, "Close My Eyes Forever." This #8 U.S. hit became the highest-charting single of both rockers' careers.

For gear, Ford rocked an Explorer-shaped Hamer Standard during her Runaways days but converted to pointy axes in the solo era. Regarding her favorite guitar, she further told Paul Rigg, "It [was] an old '80s B. C. Rich. [Company founder] Bernie Rico . . . made the most incredible guitars and I was his girl. So anything they developed and created I would play because it was absolutely what I wanted. They were original, they weren't a Telecaster or a Stratocaster copy . . . I wanted to be a leader, original and unique, and [B. C.] Rich gave me that opportunity. One day I wanted a white double neck, but the Rich Bich double necks were so big I couldn't reach the bottom neck, so they made me a smaller version of the same guitar. It is a prototype . . . [with] a preamp in the bottom neck. It is a beautiful instrument." ⚡

THE RUNAWAYS LAUNCHED THE CAREERS OF TWO GENUINE ROCK STARS.

six-string runs; just an elemental use of the guitar, much like a typical AC/DC rocker. She stuck with that winning formula for snarling hits "Bad Reputation" and 1988 comeback "I Hate Myself for Loving You."

For her instrument, Jett chose an unusual axe—a 1968 Gibson Melody Maker double-cutaway. She bought it from pop-rock pioneer Eric Carmen, who played it on a number of Raspberries hits, including the 1972 hit "Go All the Way" (it was Carmen

change, "I love Steve Vai, don't get me wrong, he is awesome; but I grew up with the riff, with Black Sabbath, Deep Purple, Richie [sic] Blackmore, and the solos."

Her platinum breakthrough was the 1988 release *Lita*, a glossy album that found a willing MTV audience for Ford's guitar flash, catchy material, and sexy videos. The first single, "Kiss Me Deadly," was a blast of metallic power pop with her shred solo at the end. Ford scored a follow-up

LEFT: JOAN JETT ON THE SET OF THE "BAD REPUTATION" VIDEO SHOOT IN 1983.
RIGHT: LITA FORD PERFORMS WITH HER B. C. RICH IN STUTTGART, GERMANY, 1988.

BRAD GILLIS & JEFF WATSON

There was moment when Night Ranger was one of the hottest guitar bands of the 1980s. With the two-headed axe monster of Brad Gillis and Jeff Watson, the band dropped the albums *Dawn Patrol*, *Midnight Madness*, and *7 Wishes*, each laden with sharp hooks, solid songwriting, and an inferno of solos. They freely combined pop melodies with metal riffs and electronic keyboards, shaping Night Ranger into an MTV-ready concoction for fans in the United States—and Japan, where they earned a rabid following.

With bassist/singer Jack Blades writing most of the material, Gillis (born June 15, 1957) and Watson (born November 5, 1956) had plenty of room to grind their chops. Of the pair, Watson was more of a Euro-metal speedster, burning up and down scales in a manner reminiscent of UFO's Michael Schenker, with blasts of Eddie Van Halen, Allan Holdsworth, and Steve Morse. His much-admired parlor trick was an *eight*-fingered tapping technique that took center stage on "(You Can Still) Rock in America," delivering a sound like a synthesizer's arpeggio

function yet at a blindingly fast tempo. Watson told the author in 1992, "I was real fortunate to get known for that eight-finger technique. It was the first time anybody had done that on video—and it established me as a player with an identity."

Prior to Night Ranger's platinum run, Brad Gillis landed one of the most daunting gigs ever, backing Ozzy Osbourne after Randy Rhoads's tragic death in March 1982. His playing on Ozzy's *Speak of the Devil* live album, in hindsight, revealed Gillis as more than up to the task. After rejoining Night Ranger, he deployed whammy dives, tapped notes, and legato runs from the southern California school of Van Halen and Rhoads. The band laid it on thick for the syrupy power ballad "Sister Christian"—and it worked. The single blew up the charts in 1984, hitting #5 and letting AM pop listeners revel in a gripping Gillis solo. Another stellar break was his sultry first lead in "Passion Play," followed by another Watson barnburner.

In Night Ranger's heyday, Watson rocked a black Les Paul Custom and a gold-sparkle Les Paul Standard

with a black pickguard. Gillis is best known for his trademark axe, a heavily modded red Fender Stratocaster, telling Willie Mosley in *Vintage Guitar Magazine*: "In '79, my brother's friend gave me a beat up '62 Strat, sanded down, in a box. It was all torn apart, but it's the guitar I rebuilt and I'm still playing today—it's my main Strat, with a built-in Nady wireless and a very original Floyd Rose non-fine-tuner model. I had an auto body shop paint it red, with leftover paint from my Datsun 240Z."

Night Ranger ran out of gas at the end of the decade, as tastes moved away from hair metal and toward the fiercer sounds of Guns N' Roses and Metallica. Yet for a few years, they were a platinum phenomenon; and Gillis and Watson became known as daring guitar heroes—foreshadowing the shred phenomenon of the late 1980s. ⚡

NIGHT RANGER DROPPED ALBUMS LADEN WITH SHARP HOOKS, SOLID SONGWRITING, AND AN INFERNO OF SOLOS.

MICK MARS

Like Kiss a decade earlier, Mötley Crüe was a quartet that earned a global fanbase, sold millions of albums and concert tickets—but never earned much respect from rock critics. In the Crüe's case, their innate ability to write a catchy metal track and deliver that monster groove onstage was overshadowed by carnival-like live shows and tabloid offstage drama. Similarly guitarist Mick Mars has never gotten much attention as a player, though the fact remains that he's a quintessential 1980s metalman and can drop a power-chord riff as heavy as anything from

electric blues. For that reason, his Crüe work is exemplified by relatively simple, soulful leads and a muscular rhythm style that grooved precisely with Nikki Sixx's bass and Tommy Lee's drums.

Mars told Joe Bosso of Music Radar, "I never got in this to be the fastest guy around. I love the blues, man . . . [and] was lucky enough to hear the blues early on. Right about the time I was starting high school we moved from Indiana to Garden Grove, California. . . . I started hanging out with a pretty cool crowd [who] turned me on to R&B, funk, soul, gospel even.

A QUINTESSENTIAL 1980s METALMAN WHO CAN DROP A RIFF AS HEAVY AS ANYTHING.

Metallica or Guns N' Roses—two bands *directly* influenced by the sound of Mötley Crüe.

While not a significant innovator, Mars (born May 4, 1951) was all about tone and rhythm. He helped carve out the California metal sound, using a supersaturated amp tone, chunky riffs, and a variety of whammy and tapping tricks. Mars—who was older than the other Crüe members—had also learned to play guitar during the 1960s guitar explosion and was drawn to the exploding sounds of

. . . But the thing I loved the most was the blues. The Paul Butterfield Blues Band's first album, that record spoke to me like a secret language only I could understand. Songs like 'Born in Chicago' and 'Thank You Mr Poobah'—that was the sh*t. . . . What a great album."

Across the 1980s, Mötley Crüe released metal singles that were custom made for MTV, combining a high-voltage show with outlandish makeup, strip-club dancers, and biker fashion. Beneath the theater,

however, was a rock-solid band that knew how to lay down a relentless beat. Cuts like "Smokin' in the Boys Room," "Home Sweet Home," and "Kickstart My Heart" (about bassist Nikki Sixx's heroin overdose) became instant staples, thanks in good measure to producer Tom Werman, who knew how to capture thick, distorted guitar and an unstoppable rhythm section on tape. To up the ante, they brought in Bob Rock to produce 1989's "Dr. Feelgood," an anthem with definitive chord chugging and Marshall tone. As far as riffage, it may be Mars's finest hour of metaldom.

For gear, Mars used a variety of Kramer and Charvel super-strats and custom-tele planks in Mötley Crüe's heyday. Yet he also grabbed plenty of Fender Stratocasters, some vintage and others modded with J. M. Rolph pickups and Floyd Rose tremolo bridges. His amp army included gear from Marshall, Soldano, Rivera, and VHT. ⚡

MICK MARS OF MÖTLEY CRÜE TAKES THE STAGE WITH ONE OF HIS STRATOCASTERS DURING THE BAND'S 2005 TOUR.

JOHN SYKES

Shred was not a well-known guitar movement in 1983—but apparently, no one gave John Sykes the memo. In his breakout performance on Thin Lizzy's *Thunder and Lightning* album, the twenty-three-year-old axeman plastered wall-to-wall notes on his black Les Paul, flat-out shredding in "Cold Sweat" before the '80s guitar style even had a name. It was like a bomb going off.

Strongly influenced by the powerhouse chops of Gary Moore, Sykes torched the rest of Thin Lizzy's final studio album, dropping fiery leads and riffs into "Holy War" and—one of the most explosive guitar tracks in the entire Lizzy catalog—"Baby, Please Don't Go." Of Thin Lizzy's final era, prior to the death of frontman Phil Lynott, Sykes told Mick Burgett of Metal Express Radio, "[The music] was a little heavier and I think that was something that I'd

Whitesnake, led by ex-Deep Purple singer David Coverdale. He appeared on the U.S. version of *Slide It In*, first augmenting—and then entirely replacing—the guitar team of Micky Moody and Mel Galley. For the 1987 *Whitesnake* album, Sykes had become Coverdale's full writing partner, heard in the hard-rock masterwork, "Still of the Night." Their Led Zeppelin influences were on full view in the vocals, Sykes's molten riffs, and a brief solo of frightening velocity. The album sold 8 million copies in the United States and put Whitesnake on top of the '80s hair-metal scene.

For gear, Sykes (born July 29, 1959) is universally identified with his 1978 Gibson Les Paul Custom, a tour-ravaged black beauty with plenty of battle wounds, and a stack of tube amps from Marshall and Mesa/Boogie. His gigantic tone on

type of sound more than a late '80s thing, and Bob's into early Purple and Zeppelin, so it was great."

However, by the time the fabled *Whitesnake* album was released, John Sykes had already been acrimoniously fired and replaced by Adrian Vandenberg and Dio's Vivian Campbell (who himself was fired a year later). Then a rising artist in his own right, Sykes parlayed this success into fronting his own power trio, Blue Murder, releasing albums in 1989 and 1993. Of special note was their '93 track "We All Fall Down," with its blinding solo, full of shred runs and pinch harmonics. Yet in the age of '90s grunge and alternative rock, the sound of glam metal was over and the cut did not get much traction on radio.

In 1996 John Sykes joined with guitarist Scott Gorham to reactivate Thin Lizzy for a number of well-received tours, all in homage to the late, great frontman Phil Lynott. Two recent solo releases include the 2021 singles "Dawning of a Brand New Day" and "Out Alive," each replete with Sykes's manic power chords, sing-along choruses—and those lethal metal solos.

SYKES DROPPED ONE OF THE MOST EXPLOSIVE GUITAR TRACKS IN THE ENTIRE LIZZY CATALOG.

brought to the table. I was into a lot of the harder guitar players in those days and I think that was something that Thin Lizzy wanted to get back to. . . . It gave it more of an edge. . . . We started digging in hard, you know."

Thin Lizzy folded the following year, but on the strength of his performance, the guitarist was able to make the critical jump to

the *Whitesnake* album, recorded in Vancouver, Canada, remains a thing of crunchy wonder, something Sykes attributed to the skills of engineer Bob Rock (Metallica, Mötley Crüe). He told Steve Newton of earofnewt. com, "Bob . . . actually created my guitar sound on the *Whitesnake* album, and we've been friends ever since. I wanted to go for an early '70s

VERNON REID

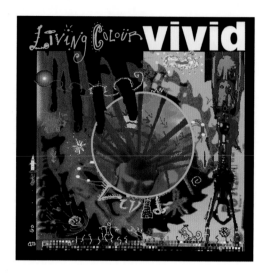

The 1988 arrival of Living Colour was a watershed moment in heavy rock, closing the decade with an eruption of guitar volcanics. Their hit "Cult of Personality" was a hit on MTV and a cultural game-changer, showcasing an African American hard rock band—and kicking down any number of preconceptions. Guitarist Vernon Reid was just as genre-pushing, as he fused free jazz, metal, funk, and shred with concepts from his days in New York's avant-garde scene. Without doubt, "Cult" has one of the most radical, explosive solos of the 1980s.

Breaking down Reid's influences helps us understand his bold approach, which eschewed polished tricks in favor of rough, expressive bends and intentionally making *noise* a part of his six-string style. While there were obvious blasts of Jimi Hendrix, Jeff Beck, and Eddie Van Halen, Reid also absorbed the

Carlos Santana coming over the radio, and I thought his guitar sounded like singing, like a vocal to me . . . [and Jimi Hendrix] was so colorful, and he kinda defined the age in a way. The whole idea of freedom and exploration, and transformation—you know, it's what united him to [John] Coltrane. Coltrane and Hendrix made very different music, but there's a point where they almost overlap."

"Cult of Personality" appeared on Living Colour's debut album, *Vivid*, which reached #6 on the Billboard 200 chart. The success of their MTV video also earned the band the opportunity to perform on *Saturday Night Live*, before a televised audience of millions, and land a coveted opener slot on The Rolling Stones' 1989 *Steel Wheels* tour (Mick Jagger was a strong early supporter of Living Colour). *Vivid* went double platinum, while their sophomore set, 1990's *Time's Up*, earned the

REID ESCHEWED POLISH IN FAVOR OF EXPRESSIVE BENDS AND INTENTIONAL NOISE.

sounds of John Coltrane, Sun Ra, James Brown, Parliament/Funkadelic, guitarist Sonny Sharrock, and Miles Davis—particularly the latter's hard-funk albums with guitar players Pete Cosey and Reggie Lucas.

Of his motivations to become a guitar player, Reid (born August 22, 1958) told S. H. Fernando Jr. of Red Bull Music Academy, "I had heard

band a Grammy award for Best Hard Rock Performance.

A noted gearhead, Vernon Reid is known for possessing one of the largest pedalboards on the planet, loaded with an army of stompboxes, pedals, MIDI foot controllers, and virtual guitar modelers for live work. For guitars, he's used a PRS Vela solidbody, a custom Hamer, and

his own signature Parker axe over the years but is best known for ESP super-strats—particularly the mid-1980s one with a swirly, psychedelic-green finish.

In an interview with the guitar company, Reid remembered, "The ESP had replaced my 'franken-strat.' One of the first photos of me in *Rolling Stone* was with a picture of this instrument. The ESP coming into my life at that point was a shift. . . . [Living Colour] was a colorful band name; I thought I should have a colorful guitar, right? The other thing about it is that 'Cult of Personality' was written on *that* guitar . . . that first riff, the whole thing. . . . 'Cult' was written in one rehearsal [which] was unusual because the entire rehearsal was dedicated to writing that one thing. We started without any ideas and ended with 'Cult.' Corey [Glover, vocalist] started singing this thing, and I yelled to Will [Calhoun, drummer] to play a beat! The song wrote itself. A few days later, we went to [legendary New York City club] CBGB's and played it for the first time." ⚡

A NOTED GEARHEAD, VERNON REID HAS USED VARIOUS SOLIDBODIES BUT IS BEST KNOWN FOR SUPER-STRATS.

The Beatles' arrival in America, followed a few years later by Eric Clapton and Jimi Hendrix, touched off a guitar boom as countless kids grabbed their first electric guitars. In 1978 a young wizard named Eddie Van Halen relit that torch for younger players—to the point where you'd have imagined heavy guitar had reached its zenith. Yet in the mid-1980s, a new generation of players arrived, igniting one of the loudest axe-travaganzas of all time: *shred*.

The pop-culture forces of MTV, the rise of guitar magazines and instructional videos, and higher-visibility touring pushed guitar to its apex, bringing forth guitarists possessing the maximum degree of technique and bravado. The precedents for shred were already there—John McLaughlin, Al Di Meola, Alvin Lee, Frank Zappa, Uli Roth, and Steve Morse had long broken the speed barrier in rock, while Van Halen and

Allan Holdsworth conjured precise whammy work, two-handed tapping, and legato. Waiting in the wings was a new fad called "sweep picking."

By 1984 guitarists like Alex Lifeson, Gary Moore, and Steve Stevens were hinting at faster things to come. Soon word of a young, Swedish ace was starting to filter out to the guitar press, with the at-first-unpronounceable name of Yngwie Malmsteen. Within two years, Yngwie—who only needed his first name by that point—was the most outrageous guitarist on Earth, following swiftly by fretburners like Steve Vai, Joe Satriani, and Eric Johnson. Elsewhere impresario Mike Varney started a guitar label called Shrapnel, specializing in baroque-infused shredders, some who became heroes (Tony MacAlpine, Jason Becker, Paul Gilbert) and others disappearing into the metallic mist (Joey Tafolla, Bernd Steidl, and underrated players like James Byrd and Michael Lee Firkins).

Looking back, shred was something of a musical schism, the moment when technique-oriented metalers broke away from heavy, blues-based guitar. Today, there are throngs of shred guitarists in just about every country, playing neoclassical, progressive, black metal, and other forms of relentless, high-velocity guitarmanship.

No question—shred is here to stay. ⚡

YNGWIE MALMSTEEN

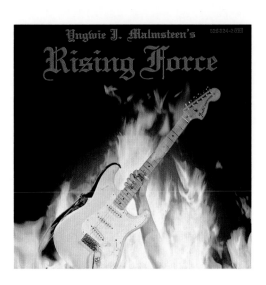

You can't utter the word *shred* without thinking of Yngwie Malmsteen—he is the living face of the genre. His arrival in the mid-1980s was an earthquake, as the Swede launched solos of blinding ferocity and heralded the coming guitar rebellion. After exploratory moves with Steeler and Alcatrazz, his early Polydor albums *Rising Force* (1984) and *Marching Out* (1985) marked a paradigm shift of six-string technique, as the twenty-something guitarist combined fast up-and-down picking, legato, and sweep picking with effortless virtuosity. Metal guitar was never the same again.

The quintessential Yngwie moment, "Black Star," remains a master class of neoclassical shred, with a dramatic instrumental groove, soaring melody, and whiplash solos at 90 mph. The influences were obvious: Ritchie Blackmore and Scorpions'

For instruments, Yngwie (born June 30, 1963) has made modified Fender Stratocasters his main axe for forty years. In an interview at his home studio, he told the author, "I have about 200 guitars in the house right now. This one here is the '71, seen on the cover of that first album, *Rising Force*. I've had it forever, but it still plays well; like most of my Strats, I had the fingerboard scalloped, put in DiMarzio HS-3 stacked humbuckers and extra-jumbo frets. I also have one of the first Strats ever built. It's dated under the neck but was refinished in black at some point. The exact date is March 3, 1954."

If Yngwie has a flaw, it's his inability to move past the baroque-metal sound he invented, a formula he's mined for decades. Each one of his solo albums sounds more or less like the one before it, making those earliest recordings

to use 50-watt Marshall MKII heads made from 1969 to 1973. People think that all Marshalls made during this period are hand-wired, but actually they're all different. I know because [company founder] Jim Marshall and I got drunk one night and he told me they just didn't give a f*ck back then. When they ran out of one capacitor or transformer, they just threw in whatever was lying around. I drive the front [the Marshall's preamp] with a Tube Screamer and Boss Noise Suppressor NS-3 and get a really warm tone."

Today Yngwie has a huge global following, notably in Japan, Eastern Europe, and home country of Sweden. For all the excesses of his playing, Yngwie is a principled guitarist who never sacrifices tone for gimmicks. Of his metallized sound, he observed, "With the Stratocaster's single-coil pickups, it's like, 'Hey, you can't hide behind a humbucker's tone, so how good are you?' Blackmore, Hendrix, and Uli Roth are all evidence of this. The single-coil sound is stripped down and allows more of the fingers and technique to show through. It's a weird thing—but I really believe it to be true." ⚡

YNGWIE STILL BRINGS IT ONSTAGE, DELIVERING SALVOS OF NOTES AND RIFFS.

Uli Roth figured prominently, along the psychedelic assault of his hero Hendrix. Yngwie applied dark minor and diminished modes, with his mile-wide vibrato, while "tricks" (such as two-handed tapping) were almost beneath him. Another track, "Far Beyond the Sun," was up-tempo metal—a modern equivalent of Niccolò Paganini's classical violin wizardry—but heard through a Stratocaster, overdrive pedal, and cranked Marshall half-stack.

the only ones of historical merit. Of course, that doesn't diminish his influences upon generations of players, from late 1980s axemen like Tony MacAlpine and Vinnie Moore to 21st-century shredders such as Nevermore's Jeff Loomis and Alexi Laiho of Children of Bodom.

Clad in ubiquitous black leather, Yngwie still brings it onstage, delivering salvos of notes and riffs from his Fenders and wall of Marshalls. Of his gear, he continued, "I prefer

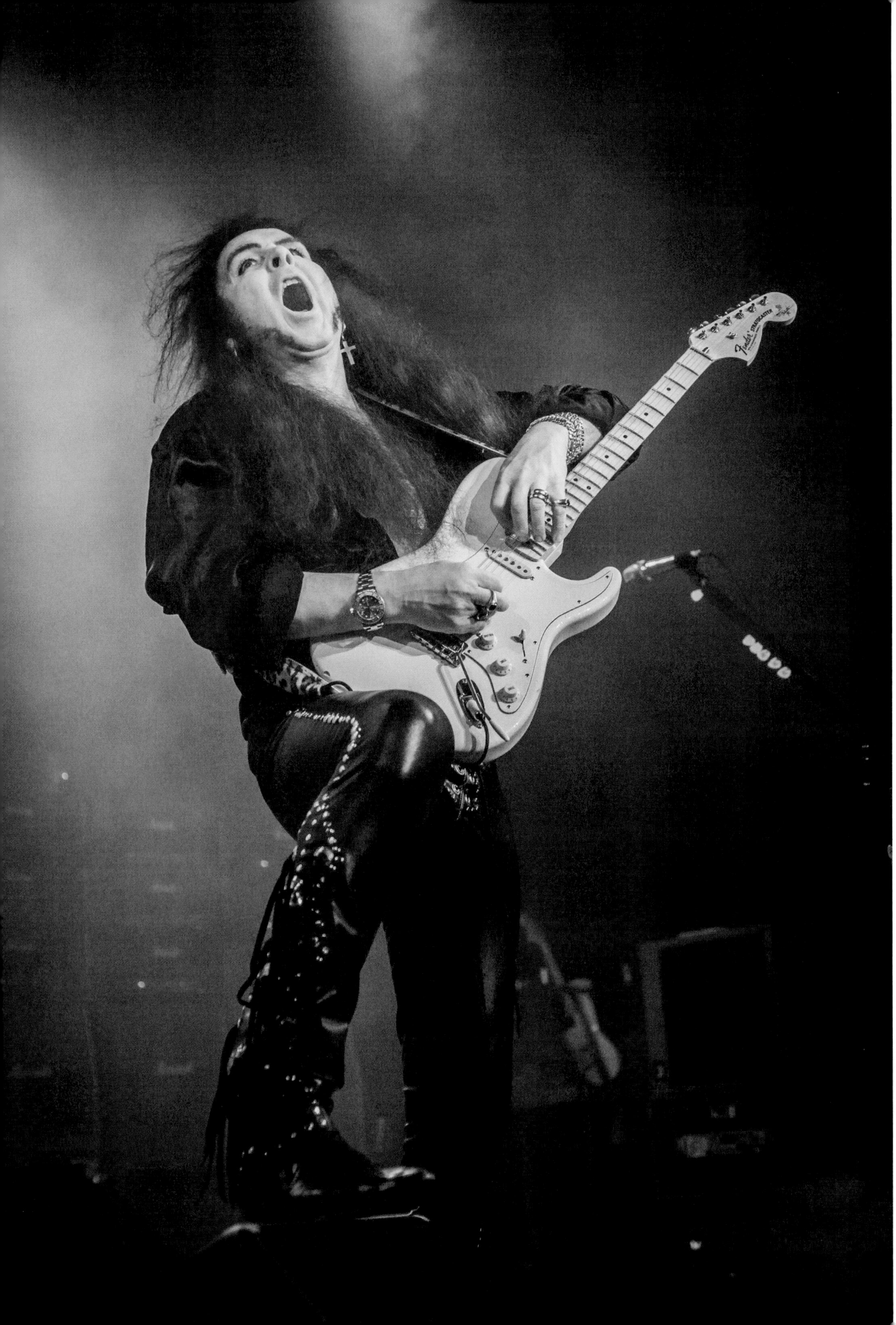

STEVE VAI

Steve Vai is the shredder almost *everyone* can agree on. He's heavy enough to appeal to metal fans but melodic enough for the classic-rock crowd. Plus the Long Island–born guitarist has a résumé that's hard to rival, playing with Frank Zappa, David Lee Roth, and Whitesnake in the 1980s before striking gold with his giga-selling *Passion & Warfare* album and ongoing G3 tours with his former guitar teacher, Joe Satriani. The dude has a terrifying array of guitar techniques—alternate-picking shred, tapping, legato, whammy dives from hell—but always deploys them in a musical way. The man never shreds for its own sake.

Vai (born June 6, 1960) first came to attention as Frank Zappa's protégé in 1980, adding so-called "stunt guitar" that combined the advanced sight-reading skills required to play Zappa's music with the

For tone, Vai has been associated with Ibanez since the late '80s, after a few years playing Performance and Charvel super-strats. His JEM model was something entirely different, as he told Jonathan Graham of *Guitar Interactive Magazine*: "When I came out with the JEM in the beginning, just the sheer fact that I approached Ibanez and said, 'This is the guitar I want . . . oh, by the way, I want to put a monkey grip in it. And . . . I want to release it in three Day-Glo different colours; green, pink and yellow.' [They're] probably just scratching their head going, 'What the heck, man? This guy's crazy!'"

Nevertheless, the Ibanez JEM and other Steve Vai models have been steady sellers for decades, along with the other pieces of gear he endorses, like Carvin Legacy tube amplifiers and the Dunlop Bad Horsie wah-wah. But his tone was

ham sandwich. And this was not a good thing . . . [so] it was from Frank that I learned that tone was in your hands—it's in your fingers, it's in the way you're playing. It's in everything you do to approach the guitar."

Beyond his four decades of guitar acrobatics and seemingly limitless creativity, Vai is also a guitar philosopher, offering wisdom and insights into the six-string experience, specifically the nuances of vibrato. He told the author, "I believe vibrato is the heart of a note's expression, but sadly it can be underutilized and even dysfunctional at times. My circular vibrato developed when I reasoned in my head that regular rock vibrato only makes the note go natural-to-sharp, while classical-type vibrato can give you natural-to-flat to natural-to-sharp, etc. But for me, classical-style vibrato on the guitar is just not rock and roll enough; so I combined the two and get the best of both worlds with the circular vibrato. But I will employ any of them based on where I am on the neck—and how I feel the melody should speak." ⚡

VAI IS A GUITAR PHILOSOPHER, OFFERING WISDOM AND INSIGHTS.

dizzying flash of Eddie Van Halen. Many fans first heard him in *Guitar Player* magazine's flexi-disc for his track "The Attitude Song," offering a post–Van Halen view of heavy guitar, rife with jazz-rock fusion chops but tailored for the 1980s. Coupled with another flexi-disc called "Blue Powder," an intense ballad with daredevil runs, a balance of distorted and clean sections, and truly spectacular harmonies, a new guitar ace had unquestionably arrived.

a work in progress that Vai started working on during his Zappa days. As Vai told Stuff.co.nz, "I hooked up with Zappa—it's 1980 and I [could] play pretty good, I guess. But I had terrible tone. . . . But I could play weird and wild, and I got the feeling that Frank liked that. . . . I remember that after our first show we're having breakfast the next day and I had to ask Frank how it went. . . . Frank said that I needed to work on my tone. He told me my tone was like *an electric*

JOE SATRIANI

Most people had never heard of Joe Satriani before Steve Vai casually dropped his name as the next big thing in electric guitar. Today Satch is an international guitar icon, but his success wasn't overnight—Satriani had to pay the studio bills for his debut album using a credit card. Fortunately the follow-up *Surfing with the Alien* album—and critical cut "Satch Boogie"—blew up at rock radio, eventually going platinum and launching the career of this instrumental shred powerhouse. Finally the guitarist could pay off his credit card bill.

What was the secret sauce behind the *Surfing* phenomenon? Satriani (born July 15, 1956) told the author, "It was a great-sounding recording of upbeat songs [and] had unexpected juxtapositions of musical composition and production styles. I grew up listening to every kind of music—classical, jazz, Motown,

Rolling Stones' Mick Jagger—not a shabby way to launch your solo career—and briefly served as Ritchie Blackmore's replacement in Deep Purple. He famously gave guitar lessons to Steve Vai and Metallica's Kirk Hammett and also had the idea to create an all-star tour called G3, featuring Vai and a revolving cast of guitar heroes. Twenty-five years later, it's still on the road. When he's not playing solo, Satriani plays with ex-Van Halen frontman Sammy Hagar in the supergroup Chickenfoot.

Behind wickedly fast hammer-ons, pull-offs, and tapping tricks, there is Satch's mile-wide dirt tone. He's widely known for his Ibanez axes, but for the *Surfing with the Alien* album, he recalled, "I used a Kramer Pacer with an original Floyd Rose trem, and two guitars I assembled from Boogie bodies and ESP parts. The throaty tone on the

sound, but with a vintage feel. I've always felt that the tone you get comes from your skin touching the fretboard, not just strings on frets. [During its development] there was a lot of input from DiMarzio [pickups] and D'Addario strings. The process went on over a couple of years. Finally, the JS models were ready."

Other tone tools in the Satch arsenal include Marshall JVM410HJ tube heads, a Vox Satchurator distortion, Dunlop wah, Digitech Whammy Pedal, Boss chorus, and a Vox Time Machine delay. For a fretburning cut like "Cool #9" from his eponymous 1995 album, tone-perfectionist Satch recalled this gear setup: "That has the chrome-top Ibanez JS on it, for that full, fat humbucker sound. For effects, I had the original Whammy Pedal, plus a Fulltone Ultimate Octave box. The wah is a Dunlop Jimi Hendrix model and those big chords that ring out are from the original demo—that's my '58 Fender Esquire through a Zoom unit. I had a lot of pedals to turn on and off, and it kept me busy—but that track was cut *live* in the studio." ⚡

BEHIND THE TAPPING TRICKS, THERE IS SATCH'S MILE-WIDE DIRT TONE.

rock and roll, funk, blues, . . . and heavy metal. I absorbed it all, and tried to remember the good bits! I like a strong melody, interesting chords, and a good groove. . . . For influences, I'd mention Chuck Berry, Hendrix, Clapton, Page, Beck, and Holdsworth. Billy Gibbons is a big influence on me and his writing with ZZ Top is so revolutionary."

Satriani's list of accomplishments is as massive as his guitar rig. In 1988 he was touring guitarist for The

title track was the Kramer into a Vox wah and a Chandler Tube Driver pedal—into a Marshall half-stack."

Satch also worked with Ibanez guitars to design a signature JS solidbody line, based on the company's Radius super-strat and still in production today. "I didn't like flat fingerboards and large frets, which was what a lot of guitars were like in those days," he told author Paul Specht in the book, *Ibanez: The Untold Story*. "I wanted a modern

JOE SATRIANI PERFORMS IN 1997.

VIVIAN CAMPBELL

Talk about luck of the Irish. This Belfast-bred shredder somehow landed in not one, but *three* giant metal acts within a single decade: Dio, Whitesnake, and Def Leppard. Of the trio, Vivian "Viv" Campbell's work with Dio remains a crucial part of 1980s metal. You can also argue that he was the first *genuine* shred guitarist to appear on a hit album, 1983's *Holy Diver*. Unlike many rippers, he didn't rely on guitar tricks like tapping and sweeping. Instead Campbell deployed the single most prevalent trait of shred—sheer picking speed—albeit with a dose of bluesy Irish soul.

Talking about his guitar influences with Willie Moseley of *Vintage Guitar Magazine*, Campbell (born August 25, 1962) said, "Rory [Gallagher] was my first guitar hero, the first concert I saw, and his live album was the first 12" record I owned. I got

were Les Paul cats, and by the time I got into [his pre-Dio band] Sweet Savage, I was a Les Paul guy."

Singer Ronnie James Dio, fresh out of Black Sabbath, put together his solo band in 1982, first with Jake E. Lee on guitar, but soon replaced by Campbell. Their debut album, 1983's *Holy Diver*, put Dio on the map with two potent singles, the Sabbath-infused title cut (conspicuously echoing Sab's "Heaven and Hell") and the radio-ready "Rainbow in the Dark." Their sophomore set, *The Last in Line*, solidified Dio's place as a potent '80s act, its title track beginning as a sweet ballad and then morphing into full metal maelstrom. Again Viv Campbell delivered the goods, blazing with unbridled fury.

Dio's 1985 *Sacred Heart* delivered another FM winner, "Rock 'n' Roll Children," and showed an increase of electronic synthesizers. Not sur-

super-strats, including one painted with the *Holy Diver* album art and fitted with Seymour Duncan pickups. Today, the guitarist presides over a line of Gibson and Epiphone Vivian Campbell signature Les Pauls.

Recalling his work on those early Dio albums, Campbell told Robert Cavuoto of My Global Mind, "[Sometimes] I cringe and think I was bending that note way to [*sic*] sharp or my vibrato was kind of nervous. . . . I'm very critical of my own performances. . . . I do think I'm a better guitar player now in a lot of ways. . . . I was always frustrated that I couldn't play like Paul Gilbert, Yngwie Malmsteen and Vinnie Moore—all these fantastically technical, proficient guitar players. I was . . . frustrated that I couldn't do sweep arpeggios or manage 54th [*sic*] note alternate picking. Now I'm happy that I can't, as my limitations on the guitar . . . helped me craft my own style, sound, and identity which I think are more important than pure technique." ⚡

CAMPBELL LANDED IN THREE GIANT METAL ACTS WITHIN A SINGLE DECADE.

into him when I was about 12, right around the time of *Irish Tour '74*. I wanted a Strat *bad*; I had a Strat copy, but I was working weekends, trying to save up money. My father finally bought me a Fender and surprised me with it. He opened up the trunk of his car, and there was a Telecaster (Thinline)—the one with the two humbuckers and an f-hole. That was my first real guitar. Then I really got into [Thin Lizzy's] Brian Robertson and Gary Moore. They

prisingly, Campbell wasn't keen with the keyboard direction and was fired during the subsequent tour. More evidence of his good fortune, Viv spent a year touring with Whitesnake, appearing in several high-profile MTV videos before finding a permanent home in Def Leppard in 1992, replacing late guitarist Steve Clark.

For guitars in the early Dio era, Campbell used a black Les Paul Standard with DiMarzio blade-style humbuckers, followed by a Charvel

VIV CAMPBELL PERFORMS WITH DIO IN LEICESTER, ENGLAND, 1984.

JASON BECKER

Barely out of high school, Jason Becker had one of metal's briefest careers, barely four years long; but he still made such an impact that guitarists are still talking about him today. As an artist on the shred-only Shrapnel Records label, Becker recorded two albums with fellow ace Marty Friedman as the duo Cacophony. The 1988 solo album *Perpetual Burn* further solidified his reputation before landing a big-ticket gig with ex–Van Halen frontman David Lee Roth. Sadly it was during those recording sessions that Becker was diagnosed with ALS, the neurodegenerative disease that ended his career.

Watching videos of the young guitarist (born July 22, 1969) reveal a teenager already in full command of the baroque-metal lexicon forged by Yngwie Malmsteen, including Becker's most famous technique—sweep picking. On his albums, you can hear

vividly heard in "Altitudes" and "Perpetual Burn," Becker said, "One day I was at a San Francisco–area subway station with Marty Friedman, waiting for our bandmates to pick us up for practice. We took out our guitars and started extending little arpeggios, one note at a time. Pretty soon we were covering every string, going up and down the neck. I went home and found that the best way to play that kind of thing was to sweep. I had never heard that term before, but it just made sense. I was lucky to have developed it with a clean and controlled sound. I often hear people trying to sweep arpeggios but can't quite nail an aggressive rhythm with it."

Tone-wise, Becker championed the wildly saturated distortion of the 1980s, using Marshall JCM800 and JCM900 heads (and occasionally a Carvin SX300H amp), with a Boss Super Distortion pedal out

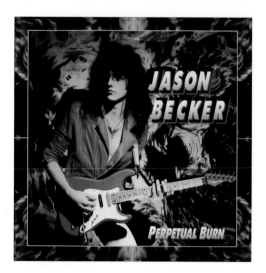

going downhill a bit, so we switched to Carvin Guitars. I asked for a blue, neck-through-body DC200 with a maple neck, and I loved what they made for me. I used the Carvin on Cacophony's album *Go Off!* and on some of Roth's *A Little Ain't Enough*."

Still his best-known guitar might be the natural-finish Peavey "Numbers" model, with big numbers actually inlaid on the fretboard. Discussing the unusual axe in 2008, Becker—who communicates through an eye-movement system developed by his father—said, "When I was in the Roth band, I got offers from many guitar companies to endorse their instruments; and I had a specific idea for the guitar I wanted. That numbered fretboard guitar was a Peavey—they nailed exactly what I had asked for and made me three versions, which I still have. [Alice Cooper guitarist] Steve Hunter and I thought of the numbers on the neck because we thought it would be funny, but I guess it can also help some people. Recently, Paradise Guitars and I have re-created that guitar. I designed the headstock myself, and the wood is alder, so it sounds sweet and thick." ⚡

VIDEOS REVEAL A TEENAGER IN FULL COMMAND OF THE BAROQUE-METAL LEXICON.

his arpeggio sweeps up and down the neck at uncanny speeds, delivering the neoclassical language of major, minor, and inevitable diminished chords. Becker studied the music of Romantic Period violinist Niccolò Paganini (1782–1840), helping develop his classically inspired style, but also cited artists diverse as Bob Dylan, Jimi Hendrix, Eric Clapton, and Eddie Van Halen.

In an interview with the author about developing his sweep style,

front to pump out the thickest gain possible. Recalling his various locking-tremolo-fitted solidbodies, he remembered, "I got a black and white Fender Stratocaster like Eric Clapton's and put a Steve Morse pickup in it. That was my main guitar through the Cacophony album *Speed Metal Symphony*. Then Marty Friedman and I endorsed a Japanese company called Hurricane Guitars; I wore it out on my album *Perpetual Burn*. After that, Hurricane started

VIDEOS OF THE YOUNG JASON BECKER REVEALED A TEENAGER IN FULL COMMAND OF THE BAROQUE-METAL LEXICON.

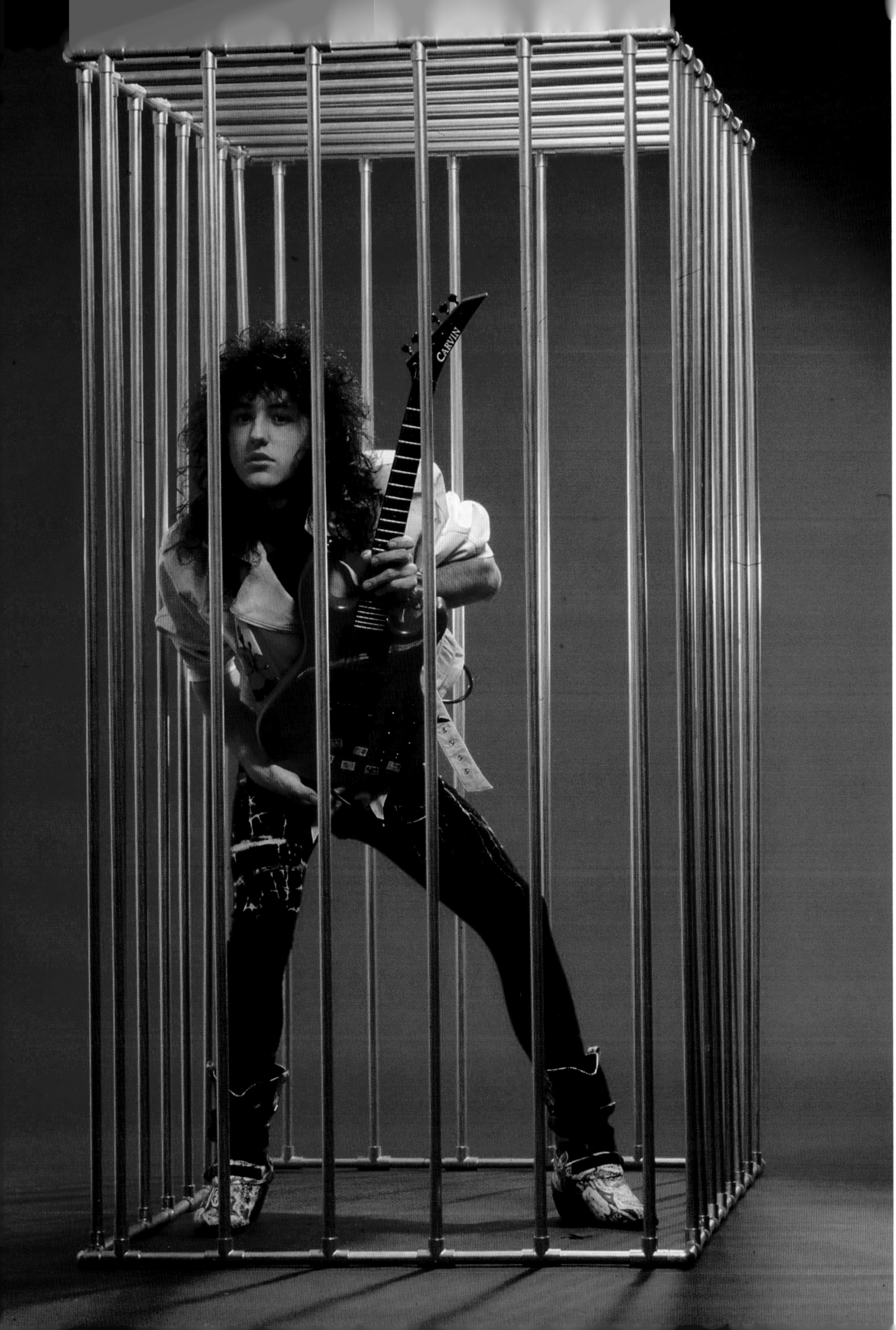
CARVIN

PAUL GILBERT

It's hard to imagine a neoclassical metal guitarist who could pick faster than, say, Yngwie Malmsteen or Tony MacAlpine—yet somehow Paul Gilbert *was* faster, his wildly exciting lines often threatening to go off the rails. As another late-'80s Shrapnel Records artist, he was a member of the first shred band, Racer X, and later went to pop-rock stardom with Mr. Big. Yet, it is Gilbert's early work that made true Bach 'n' roll history.

Still a mere teenager, Paul got his big break after sending a cassette to Shrapnel president Mike Varney. He told Ruben Mosqueda of Sleazeroxx, "Back in the day, Mike had a column in *Guitar Player* called 'Spotlight.' I had sent a tape to Mike. Randy Rhoads had passed away. I was about 15 years old at the time. I didn't know anyone in the business, but I thought, 'If I don't try, I will never get a gig like that.' So the only thing I could think of was to get a tape to

I really like your playing. Keep sending me stuff!'"

As a player, Gilbert took obvious cues from Yngwie, as well as '70s rockers Pat Travers and Robin Trower, but most from his hero Eddie Van Halen. As he told Ruben Mosqueda of SleazeRoxx, "I have so many memories of picking up those early Van Halen records. I would take them, listen to them, and try to dissect them. They were my homework assignment. Everyone knows about his tapping, but a lot of the stuff that I learned from Eddie's playing was the fingerpicking, like you hear on 'Little Guitars' or on 'Bottoms Up.' There would be people at the guitar shops playing Eddie Van Halen, but they wouldn't be able to capture that vibrato. It was like getting a mouthful of icing, but they were missing the cake! That's the best part! Eddie played with the energy of a kid, but the grip of a grown-up."

fying scalar assaults, at ridiculous tempos. The band's greatest track is "Scarified," a three-headed monster of neoclassical bombast—it's one of the purest examples of Bach 'n' roll ever recorded and a stupefying demonstration of shred. (Racer X also launched the career of Scott Travis—Judas Priest's powerhouse drummer since 1989.)

For guitars, Paul Gilbert has been an Ibanez endorser for thirty years, with his signature PGM models—super-strats with decorative f-holes—and the Fireman model, which resembles a flipped-over Ibanez Iceman with a new cutaway notch. As Gilbert told Benjamin Delacous of Hardforce.com, "The neck of these [Fireman] guitars is very thick, they give a good sustain and it's easy to make bends. Also, I had a magnet mounted on the pickguard to hold my bottleneck, which is very important to me, because I often use it for my melodies. It's cool to have that sound. I can put the slide back in place easily and continue [to play] normally."

GILBERT TOOK OBVIOUS CUES FROM YNGWIE, AS WELL AS '70s ROCKERS PAT TRAVERS AND ROBIN TROWER, BUT MOST FROM HIS HERO EDDIE VAN HALEN.

someone, because I didn't have any connections. I remember Mike had printed the address and said something like that he would respond to anyone that would send him a tape. I sent him the tape and he got back to me. He said, 'Hey you're just a kid, I can't help you get the Ozzy audition.

Showing the Malmsteen influence, for Racer X's 1986 debut *Street Lethal*, Gilbert even coyly titled a track "Y.R.O." for "Yngwie rip-off." For their followup set, *Second Heat*, Gilbert and shred-bassist Juan Alderete hired another guitarist, Bruce Bouillet, for even more terri-

PAUL GILBERT WIELDS HIS SIGNATURE IBANEZ FIREMAN AXE WITH MR. BIG IN 2011.

GEORGE LYNCH

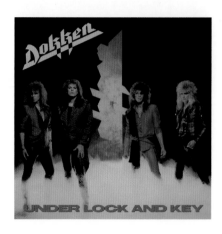

One of the legitimate heirs of Eddie Van Halen, guitarist George Lynch of Dokken had the picking speed, tricks, and rock-star looks to become a major shred figure. While several of the quartet's 1980s albums sold over 1 million copies, Dokken—itself a defining hair-metal band—never achieved top-tier status, relegating Lynch to cult heroism. Still the rocker became seriously influential. "George Lynch took the tricks and techniques of the Van Halenites, added unbridled frenzy and a seriously heavy tone," observed writer H. P. Newquist in the book *Legends of Rock Guitar*. "His impressive soloing, blistering two-handed style, and killer tone set him apart from most guitarists of the day."

To be sure, Lynch (born September 28, 1954) was an unrepentant shredder, skittering around the fretboards of his Charvel-parts "Tiger" and ESP Kamikaze solidbodies with

itable display of mach-speed picking.

For influences, Lynch told David Szabados of Legendary Tones, "I'm sort of a chameleon in the sense that I tend to acquire stuff from good players from every era. . . . I've been heavily influenced by the Beatles, Albert King, Hendrix, Page, Clapton, Beck, Johnny Winter, Leslie West, Blackmore, Gibbons, Brian May, Frank Marino, Al Di Meola, Schenker, Uli Roth, Holdsworth, EVH, Yngwie and a hundred other players from the '60s to present day. I think what I'm blessed with is the ability to take those influences, . . . [and make] it part of my musical vocabulary."

The 1985 album *Under Lock and Key* was Dokken's apex moment, using tighter arrangements, soaring vocals, and simplified riffing to achieve a Scorpions-like FM accessibility. (*Trivia:* Don Dokken had sung on the demos for Scorpions' famous

Discussing the genesis of his super-strats, the Dokken axeman recalled his first meetings with the ESP guitar company, telling Tony Bacon for Reverb, "Back then, bigger was better, heavier was better, more was more. So I said it had to be a high-gain pickup, a heavy piece of wood, very thick [with] a minimal amount of routing. And I wanted graphics: a Kamikaze pilot, some bombs, a couple of *kanji* characters. . . . I love having that single-coil, fluid kind of legato tone at the neck, and then if I want to back it off, I can get a crystalline Strat sound. . . . The wide-flat neck dimensions . . . were something that back then wasn't as common as now. . . . None of it was treading any new ground, but when you put it all together, I think it was really the predecessor to a lot of guitars."

After Dokken imploded at the end of the '80s (from notorious friction between Lynch and his frontman), the guitarist formed Lynch Mob and went on to record a number of solo albums and side projects. A renowned tone merchant, Lynch's line of Seymour Duncan Screamin' Demon replacement humbuckers remains a popular metal mod, while for amps, he's used tube heads from Marshall, Soldano, Randall, Diezel, Bogner, and others—all laden with heavy gain and delay. Not content to just be an endorser, Lynch even builds his own personally customized Mr. Scary guitars. ⚡

DOKKEN NEVER ACHIEVED TOP-TIER STATUS, RELEGATING LYNCH TO CULT HEROISM.

terrifying speed and tapping. He missed out on two auditions for Ozzy Osbourne's group (losing out to Randy Rhoads and Jake E. Lee) but finally sealed the deal with Dokken. For demonstrations of his virtuosity, listen to 1984's "Don't Close Your Eyes," where the guitarist ripped modal lines over a ferocious drumbeat. "Into the Fire" showcases more of a melodic approach—*and* that inev-

Blackout album, while frontman Klaus Meine was recovering from vocal surgery.) "Unchain the Night" had a jaw-dropping solo, while "In My Dreams" went for Def Leppard–style vocal processing over power chords and a face-melting lead. Another key performance was "Mr. Scary," an instrumental with sinister intervals and harmonies—and one of those speed-of-light Lynch solos.

TONY MACALPINE & VINNIE MOORE

After the dramatic arrival of Yngwie Malmsteen, the hunt was on for neo-classical shredders who could deliver more notes per square inch; in short order, Shrapnel Records discovered Tony MacAlpine and Vinnie Moore. Each was a technical virtuoso, capable of impossible arpeggio sweeps and alternate-picking skills to dazzle the guitar magazine masses.

MacAlpine (born August 29, 1960) was first up with his 1986 *Edge of Insanity* album, an instrumental set with one of the silliest metal-album covers ever—a cartoonish illustration of hairy, manacled feet. Fortunately the shred chops within clicked with listeners, as the Springfield, Massachusetts, axeman exhibited a full suite of classically influenced metal, already as advanced as those of Yngwie. "Wheel of Fortune" was a full baroque demonstration of

shredder used Kramer and B. C. Rich super-strats with DiMarzio pickups and mostly Peavey amplifiers. Later MacAlpine helped develop eight-string Ibanez solid-bodies, offering an expanded range of progressive-shred axemanship.

Of his guitar influences, MacAlpine told Thom Jennings of Backstageaxxess.com, "When I first started it was my brother and then Johnny Winter and George Benson. Later it was Randy Rhoads and Eddie Van Halen. I was checking them out with some of the other local players. But in reality my sound comes from my exposure to classical music at the age of five. I knew early on what I wanted to accomplish in music."

Released in August 1986, Vinnie Moore's *Mind's Eye* was another shredfest, solidifying his place among the first wave of classi-

in his career, a 1987 Ibanez VM1. In later years, the Delaware guitarist landed a prime sideman gig in the esteemed Euro-metal band UFO and served as its lead guitarist for many years. Usually Moore can be seen playing Dean Vinman 2000 super-strats using locking trem systems and an HSS configuration of DiMarzio and Dean DMT pickups.

Looking back at the dawn of shred guitar in the 1980s, Moore told the author, "I saw Al Di Meola, Paco de Lucia, and John McLaughlin at the Tower Theater near Philadelphia, around 1981 while I was in high school, and those guys blew my freakin' mind. I was also into instrumental stuff by Jeff Beck, Larry Carlton, and Carlos Santana. All of that had a huge influence on me as a player and songwriter and was the reason I went in an instrumental direction. I was also into straight rock bands like Led Zep, Deep Purple, and Van Halen, and was always more of a rock guy than anything else. So I guess if anything, I was one of the first players to record instrumental records in a *heavy rock* vein, as opposed to the jazz and fusion stuff I grew up on." ⚡

EACH IS A TECHNICAL VIRTUOSO, CAPABLE OF IMPOSSIBLE ARPEGGIO SWEEPS.

arpeggios, harmonies, and leaden riffs from bassist Billy Sheehan (David Lee Roth, Mr. Big) and drummer Steve Smith (Journey).

"Quarter to Midnight" was the all-important solo guitar extravaganza, with tapping and speed runs exploding in every direction. An equally skilled keyboardist, MacAlpine contributed a boisterous piece of Chopin on piano, the "Prelude 16, Opus 28." For gear on his early albums, the

cal-metal soloists. "In Control" has plenty of Uli Roth–style harmonies, Al Di Meola–tinged modal runs, and even keyboard work from fellow Shrapnel ace, Tony MacAlpine. "Daydream" was a power-picking thrill ride, with bassist Andy West (the Dixie Dregs) and drummer Tommy Aldridge (Ozzy Osbourne) lending heavy support.

Moore (born April 14, 1964) also received a signature guitar very early

TOP: TONY MACALPINE PERFORMS IN MOSCOW IN 2012.
BOTTOM: VINNIE MOORE APPEARS WITH UFO AT LONDON'S O2 ACADEMY IN 2010.

ARMY OF SHREDDERS

Throughout the late 1980s, *a lot* of shredders emerged from the woodwork—endless armies of them. By mid-decade, the high-technique style was dominating the guitar-o-sphere, ushering in cookie-cutter players wielding super-strats with whammy bars, wearing Spandex, and tapping to excess. But there were also key innovators and tasty soloists beyond Yngwie Malmsteen, at least until the anti-guitar-hero sounds of grunge toppled the movement in the 1990s.

The one-two punch of Eddie Van Halen and Randy Rhoads, between 1978 and 1982, touched off the phenomenon, with their advanced techniques and overt allusions to baroque-classical music. The influence of jazz-rock guitarists Al Di Meola and John McLaughlin should not be underestimated—so many shredders have acknowledged their seismic fusion chops. (In fact, while the bulk of shredders resided in the metal camp, there were a few non-metal speeders, such as Eric Johnson and the incredible Shawn Lane.)

Among the first authentic shredders out of the gate was Jake E. Lee. He won the coveted slot in Ozzy Osbourne's band and delivered fiery, non-whammy-bar thrills on "Bark at the Moon" (1983), rife with phase-shifter effects on a white Charvel axe. Ratt's *Out of the Cellar* album gave MTV an early slice of the shred pie with 1984's "Round and Round," which fused Van Halen and Judas Priest riffery into a glam-metal confection (its campy video starred '50s TV comedian Milton Berle). Lead guitarist Warren DiMartini's aggressive licks on the follow-up "Lay It Down" were the epitome of So-Cal guitar, combining speed runs with wide intervallic leaps on Charvel and Performance super-strats.

By decade's end, fretboard speeders were coming fast and furious, some more melodic and pop-informed. One-hit wonder White Lion had a major smash in 1987 with "Wait," offering a Boston-like acoustic intro before the ubiquitous Van Halen-isms of the era. It was Vito Bratta's beautiful, uncanny solo of two-handed tapping that stole the show, a true highwater mark of shred technique and style. Another poppish metal act was Winger, matching the made-for-video songwriting and hip gyrations of frontman Kip Winger with Reb Beach's insane axe work on "Seventeen." Beach later became a sought-after sideman with Whitesnake, Dokken, and Night Ranger.

Yngwie Malmsteen may be the face of shred, but Michael Angelo Batio is perhaps its quintessential stylist. From his *over/under* fretting technique to playing two-necked and even his four-necked Quad guitar, the ambidextrous Batio is shred at its most outrageous, heard on the 1989 Nitro single "Freight Train."

The Shrapnel Records label brought forth its own galaxy of fretmen, mostly neoclassical stylists (such as Tony MacAlpine and Vinnie Moore), but also funk-fusion cats Richie Kotzen and Greg Howe. Labelmate James Byrd was perhaps the most soulful of the bunch, bringing together the Euro-metal with neo-classical on his obscure, yet magnificent *Son of Man* album. Ultrafast Nuno Bettencourt combined metal, pop, and funk for Extreme, using a Washburn N4 solidbody with the Stephens Extended Cutaway for extreme upper-fret access. From Japan, Akira Takasaki made a brief noise with the perfectly named Loudness.

Shred guitar even broke into Hollywood. From the blockbuster flick *Back to the Future*, Michael J. Fox grabbed a red Gibson ES-345 in a pivotal scene and jammed on Chuck Berry–style riffs—before breaking into a tapping frenzy. For 1986's *Crossroads*, actor Ralph Macchio dueled with shred god Steve Vai for the big finale, showcasing blues slide and a hyper-metallic rendering of Niccolò Paganini's "Caprice No. 5." The blues bits were played by bottleneck master Ry Cooder; the shred parts were all Vai, then a rising guitarist with Alkatrazz.

For much of the 1980s and well into the '90s, shred simply *devoured* the guitar universe. ⚡

TOP: JAKE E. LEE IN CONCERT WITH OZZY OSBOURNE, CIRCA 1984.
BOTTOM LEFT: THE AMBIDEXTROUS MICHAEL ANGELO BATIO IS PERHAPS SHRED'S QUINTESSENTIAL STYLIST.
BOTTOM RIGHT: NUNO BETTENCOURT AND EXTREME PERFORM AT BIRMINGHAM, ENGLAND'S O2 ACADEMY IN 2014.

THRASH
SMASH
& BASH

At the same time shred was changing guitar technique, another 1980s movement was afoot—this one rattling heavy metal to its core. Unlike the melodic metal sounds of Dio and Iron Maiden, this rock was angular and unforgiving, with an emphasis on brutal grooves, tritone intervals, and drop-tuned guitar riffs. Dubbed *thrash* for its violent persona, it was a true revolution, as dramatic a sea change as the British Invasion, psychedelia, or punk.

Thrash evolved from all manner of fast, extreme hard rock, including watershed moments like Black Sabbath's "Symptom of the Universe," Queen's "Stone Cold Crazy," and Motörhead's "Ace of Spades," a cut that fused

pub rock, punk, and metal like nothing else before. During the New Wave of British Heavy Metal (circa 1979–1982), heavy bands continued pushing the limits of tempo and distortion, including Judas Priest, Saxon, and Tygers of Pan Tang. There were also rising underground metalers of all kinds—Mercyful Fate, King Diamond, Anvil, Sodom, Diamond Head, Venom, and Angel Witch—and that's barely scratching the surface.

Still it was the collective effort of thrash's "big four"—Metallica, Megadeth, Anthrax, and Slayer—that gave the movement its focus and defining style. There were other critical early bands, such as Overkill, Nuclear Assault, and Metal Church, all inciting brutal mosh pits in concert. Stylistically, each deployed shreddy guitar solos, but rhythm riffs and drums were far more important—thrash was sometimes compared to the noise of a construction-site jackhammer. Thrash's lyrics were also dark and cynical, coloring a picture of the world about to go to hell.

This new sound also necessitated new gear. For guitars, the venerable Gibson Les Paul and Fender Stratocaster solidbodies were bypassed in favor of the ubiquitous Flying V. Whether made by Gibson—or one of countless variations and *wedge*-shaped beasties crafted by ESP, Schecter, Dean, and Jackson—there was a V-wielding axeman in just about every major thrash band. As a result, the Flying V became the ultimate symbol of heavy metal guitar. ⚡

JAMES HETFIELD & KIRK HAMMETT

Metallica is the veritable King Kong of thrash. Since their 1980s arrival, the San Francisco quartet has defined the genre but took it to the top of the charts. Today, Metallica is considered the global ambassador of not just thrash but *all* heavy metal. James Hetfield and Kirk Hammett also changed the guitar lexicon, using raw-edged riffs and spastic leads to carve out new sounds previously unheard in metal circles. Along with rapid-fire drummer Lars Ulrich and aggro-bassist Cliff Burton (who tragically died in 1986), Metallica was a sonic revolution from its earliest days through their 1991 platinum peak with "The Black Album"—a self-titled disc that has since sold over 16 million copies.

Heard on the band's 1983 debut *Kill 'em All*, the building blocks of thrash were already in place, heard on "Hit the Lights," "The Four

very rhythmic, and . . . there's some great rhythm guitar players out there: Malcolm Young [of AC/DC] obviously. Rudolf Schenker [Scorpions] and I would say Johnny Ramone [The Ramones] had just a great right hand: a lot of down picking, *da-da-da-da*, really machine-like. I just gravitated toward that. And obviously the musicality of a riff: Somebody like a Tony Iommi [Black Sabbath], who is the ultimate riff master in my opinion—so a combination of heavy and great melodies within the riffs."

"Ride the Lightning," title cut of the 1984 album, found the band becoming more polished, taking the speed-freaked beats of Motörhead and Killing Joke, and adding complex sections, sinister distortion, and Hammett's proto-shred leads. "Battery" opened 1986's breakthrough *Master of Puppets*, starting with a quiet section of acoustic guitars

got a small inheritance of like maybe $150 or something. And I took that money and bought a wah pedal. And it was amazing because all of a sudden I felt like I was able to make sounds that Jimi Hendrix was making, but also sounds that Brian Robertson—the guy from Thin Lizzy—was making, that Pat Travers was making . . . the sounds that I was hearing on all these different albums. And I played that wah pedal, literally, for like months on end. People say that using wah pedal can be a crutch, and yeah, it can be, and I am certainly guilty of that, I'll admit it . . . but only because I just love it so much."

For guitars, the early Metallica records and tours found Hammett jamming on his black 1979 Gibson Flying V, while Hetfield manhandled a white Electra V copy. Later Hammett moved on to innumerable ESP super-strats (including his famed one with Boris Karloff's mummy graphic), while Hetfield gravitated to Explorers from Gibson and ESP, all backed by mountains of Mesa/Boogie tube stacks. A noted guitar collector, Hammett also owns "Greeny"—the 1959 Gibson Les Paul Standard 'burst previously owned by iconic players Peter Green and Gary Moore. ⚡

. . . A SONIC REVOLUTION FROM THEIR EARLIEST DAYS THROUGH 1991'S "THE BLACK ALBUM."

Horsemen," and especially "Motorbreath." On this last track, one can observe the fast, high-speed riffing that would influence generations of players. It's critical to remember that *every* rhythm guitar track on early Metallica albums was recorded exclusively by Hetfield (born August 3,1963). Hammett was strictly relegated to solos.

As the Metallica frontman told Jeff Perlah for *Newsweek*, "What I do is play drums on the guitar. I'm

before the inevitable wall-of-doom from Hetfield, Burton, and Ulrich. Hammett (born November 18, 1962) executed a characteristically wild solo, laced with wah-wah and overbent strings, each element contributing to Metallica's first masterpiece.

Of his trademark style, heard around the planet in the mega-hit "Enter Sandman," Hammett told GibsonTV's *Icons* show, "The very first time I got a wah pedal was because a relative of mine passed away, and I

TOP: METALLICA'S KIRK HAMMETT PLAYS THE BORIS KARLOFF GUITAR FOR FANS IN TURIN, ITALY, 2018.
BOTTOM: JAMES HETFIELD WITH ONE OF HIS FAVORED EXPLORER-STYLE GUITARS IN CHORZOW, POLAND, 2008.

DAVE MUSTAINE

If Metallica was the first band to blow up the thrash scene, Megadeth was not far behind. Frontman Dave Mustaine had been Metallica's lead guitarist prior to their first album—he was infamously fired for misbehavior—yet he went on to this platinum-encrusted second act. In contrast to the grim realism of Metallica, Megadeth's metal veered toward a campier, horror-movie approach that appealed to teenage boys the world over. Along the way, the thrash institution employed a litany of fret-flailers, including shred hero Marty Friedman, Chris Poland, Chris Broderick, and Jeff Young, all of whom shared lead duties with Mustaine.

Among the top thrash bands, Mustaine found his niche within the theatricality of shock rock. While James Hetfield's wordplay was grim and cynical, Mustaine wrote on exaggerated, B-movie subjects of

fans an alternative to the glammy hair metal of Night Ranger and Whitesnake. As proof of concept, albums like *Peace Sells . . . but Who's Buying?* (1986), *So Far, So Good . . . So What!* (1988), and *Rust in Peace* (1990) all went platinum in the United States, establishing Megadeth as one of thrash's leading forces.

On guitar, Mustaine (born September 13, 1961) was a perfect thrash hero for the '80s/'90s metal scene, wearing street jeans and T-shirts onstage and riffing on Flying V and wedge-shaped solidbodies—an echo of his teen-era influence from UFO's Michael Schenker. During the decades, Mustaine has used axes from Jackson, ESP, Dean, and Gibson, along with Marshall amps and endorsed stompboxes, like the Zoom G2.1DM multi-effects unit. His suite of pointy signature guitars has included the Jackson KV1, ESP

moving two-note power chord, but with a minor-sixth bass note inserted between beats, using the middle finger. For primo thrash guitar, "Holy Wars . . . The Punishment Due" from *Rust in Peace* is a definitive track. Its brutal chord riff captures their saturated-distortion, rhythmic style, as well as virtuoso solos from Marty Friedman and the frontman.

Of that acclaimed stomper, Mustaine told Spencer Kaufman of Heavy Consequence, "If I have a song and I have an idea for something and I hear a solo, I've always said, 'There's their way, our way, and my way.' What that means is, when it comes to solo time, I'll say, 'Okay, go ahead [and do it your way].' If it's great, it's great. Marty pulled that off a lot of times. Not a lot of the players have had their very first solo be the keeper solo. I mean, in all the songs I've played on—almost 200—I've only had one song *ever* . . . where I kept the first solo I played, and that was in 'Holy Wars.'"

MUSTAINE POSSESSES A TOOLBOX OF PERIOD-CORRECT LEAD AND RHYTHM CHOPS, THOUGH IS ACKNOWLEDGED FOR HIS "SPIDER CHORD."

insanity ("Sweating Bullets"), death and war, Satanism ("The Conjuring"), and aliens, accompanied by the cartoonish cover art typical of 1980s metal albums. Musically their brand of crunch mixed Euro-metal with high-speed punk riffing, offering

DV8, Dean VMNT, and Gibson Dave Mustaine Flying V EXP.

Regarding technique, the Megadeth man possesses a toolbox of period-correct lead and rhythm chops, though acknowledged for his so-called "spider chord." This is a

KERRY KING & JEFF HANNEMAN

If every thrash group's goal is to be *heavier* than the band before it, the 1980s champion would inevitably be Slayer. Their brand of speed metal was the equivalent of a slasher movie, with bassist Tom Araya's vocals about doom, murder, and war—and *worse*—matched by the ungodly guitar assault of Kerry King and Jeff Hanneman, and Dave Lombardo's industrial-strength drums. While there were lots of dark, formidable bands in that era, Slayer was the heaviest of the heavy.

Their now-landmark *Reign in Blood* album was issued in 1986 with producer Rick Rubin at the helm, and it transformed metal with its savage attack and grim lyrics. Clocking in at a mere 29 minutes, the album was metal in its purest form, with no concessions to melody or radio accessibility. Inspired by metal, the dark side of humanity, and *lots* of hardcore punk, Slayer's style emphasized brutal

started writing [Slayer] music . . . I knew most people weren't going to get it. But we started growing this army of fans. Kerry and I would work in the studio saying, 'What riff do you have? Let's put it together with this riff.' The songs we play most are 'Angel of Death' and 'Raining Blood.' No matter how many times we play them, they're still exciting; the kids go nuts. They're two great songs and are fun to play."

Slayer's backline was the inevitable wall of Marshall JCM800 heads and cabinet stacks. Regarding his early years and guitars—usually B. C. Rich Warlock and Kerry King V models—Kerry King (born June 3, 1964) told The Music Zoo, "When I was thirteen, my dad wanted to keep me out of trouble, so I started playing. [For gear], I was with B. C. Rich until 1989–90, but the company was sold—I had them make me a

to relearn how to play to use a Floyd Rose; the Kahler is flat [to the body]."

Hanneman used B. C. Rich Bich and Gunslinger models and a Jackson Soloist early on but later switched to a range of custom ESP super-strats. He noted, "[For guitars], my favorite thing to do is get a black guitar and put white punk stickers on it. ESPs have always been great guitars; when I'm standing onstage, it feels part of me."

For Slayer's last concert on November 30, 2019, the remaining members acrimoniously announced they were breaking up and would never play together again. On their official Twitter page, a final message—written in a perfectly morose thrash tone—was posted, saying: "Slayer nation, at this very moment thousands of fans inside the Forum in LA are counting down to the final sold-out show of Slayer's Final World Tour. . . . [as] we bid farewell to the long-reigning titans of thrash. This is the end of the monsters." ⚡

SLAYER'S STYLE EMPHASIZED BRUTAL RHYTHMS AND DISTORTED CHORD-CHUGGING OVER EVERYTHING ELSE.

rhythms and distorted chord-chugging over everything else. The tracks "Angel of Death" and "Raining Blood" remain classics of the genre, both played at terrifying tempos.

As the late Hanneman (1964–2013) told ESP Guitars, "When we

nice Mockingbird, but I didn't have the money to pay for it. So they sold it! Then I went to ESP for ten years but went back to B. C. Rich. I use Kahler tremolos because I could never understand why anyone would cut the back of a string off. I'd have

SLAYER'S JEFF HANNEMAN AND KERRY KING DURING THEIR ESP DAYS, 1991.

SCOTT IAN

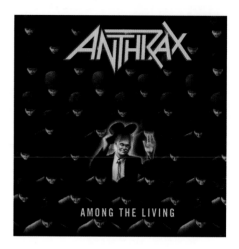

Anthrax is one of the core groups that helped determine the trajectory of the entire thrash genre. Unlike West Coast bands like Metallica, Megadeth, Testament, and Slayer, Anthrax is a resolutely New York institution, representing the East Coast along with bands like Overkill, Agnostic Front, and Nuclear Assault. More than just thrash, they also wove in rap textures, just as the Beastie Boys were doing with hardcore '80s punk. This hip-hop flavor, mixed with its punk-metal crossover, gave Anthrax an attack like no other.

monies of the Allman Brothers Band and Thin Lizzy, with Spitz taking a uniquely layered guitar solo.

Spitz played on all of Anthrax's early albums, but quit in the 1990s to become, surprisingly, a master Swiss-watch artisan. Subsequent albums featured a revolving case of guest and semipermanent lead players, including Paul Crook, the late Dimebag Darrell (Pantera), Rob Caggiano (Volbeat), and Jon Donais (Shadows Fall). Through it all have been the persistent thud riffs—and lyrics—of rhythm guitarist Scott Ian.

UNLIKE WEST COAST THRASH BANDS, ANTHRAX IS A RESOLUTELY NEW YORK INSTITUTION, REPRESENTING THE EAST COAST ALONG WITH BANDS LIKE OVERKILL, AGNOSTIC FRONT, AND NUCLEAR ASSAULT.

The quintet's big break was 1987's *Among the Living* album, with tracks like "Caught in a Mosh" and "I Am the Law" revealing the twin-guitar stomp of Scott Ian—the only constant member in the band's history—and lead guitarist Danny Spitz (both guitarists born in 1963). The album's guitar/bass/drum sonics were abetted by legendary producer Eddie Kramer (Jimi Hendrix, Led Zeppelin, Kiss, Peter Frampton). "Efilnikufesin (N.F.L.)" has sick guitar harmonies, far different from the traditional har-

Regarding his hybrid tastes in metal and hip-hop, Ian told Brad Sanders of *Stereogum*, "I f*cking loved hip-hop early on, and most of my friends did not. When Iron Maiden's *Killers* came out, I was also listening to Grandmaster Flash. When *Number of The Beast* came out, I was listening to Run-D.M.C. So yeah, I didn't get it. I didn't understand why everyone I knew in the rock and metal world didn't feel hip-hop the same way I felt it. Why wasn't rap music moving people the same way it

moved me? Why weren't they hearing the same aggression in it that I was hearing? I could listen to Agnostic Front or I could listen to Venom or I could listen to, you know, LL Cool J, and they were all moving me in the same way. There was an aggression there. There was a link for me in my brain, my heart, whatever."

A diehard user of Jackson ATL Soloist super-strat and King V solidbodies (with Randall amps), Ian told David Slavkovi⊠ of Ultimate-Guitar.com why he uses Jacksons: "You know, there's other brands that work too, but there's just something about the Jackson sound. I think a lot of it has to do with the fact that the guy that built my first-ever Jackson—his name is Mike Shannon—he runs a custom shop for Jackson in California—the first Jackson I ever owned was a 1982 Randy Rhoads model which I bought at Sam Ash . . . it took about eight months for it to come, but it was well worth the wait. You could see pictures of that guitar on old Anthrax records, it was my No. 1 guitar for many years. And the man who built that guitar was Mike Shannon—and [he's] still building my Jacksons. It's the same guy running the custom shop, doing it on the same old machines that he did back then." ⚡

ANTHRAX'S SCOTT IAN IS A DIE-HARD USER OF JACKSON ATL SOLOIST SUPER-STRAT AND KING V SOLIDBODIES.

EXTENDED RANGE GUITARS

As thrash evolved, so too did its instruments. With the arrival of heavy bands like King's X and, later, Alice in Chains, guitarists discovered a range of new sounds under the umbrella term of "drop tuning," the act of detuning strings into deep, murkier territory. If could be as simple as drop-D—the common folk tuning of D-A-D-G-B-E—or even tuning even lower. Around 1990, Steve Vai worked with Ibanez to develop its Universe series of seven-string solidbodies, opening the door to everyone who wanted to explore the world of "extended range" guitars. Built by multiple companies, these instruments later included eight- and even nine-string guitars, as well as six-string baritones with longer necks. The trend launched a whole new generation of electric solidbody guitars.

Within a few years, drop-tuned players could be found all over metal, notably the guitarists Munky and Head of Korn. Their hybrid of hard rock and rap coalesced into a groove-oriented genre called *nü-metal*, which drew big crowds—and hostility from mainstream metalers who rejected its heavy drums, slick production, and hip-hop emphasis. You can hear Munky and Head's seven-string tones in '90s Korn hits "Freak on a Leash" and "Blind," both featuring subatomic riffs in the dropped-A tuning of A-D-G-C-F-A-D. Noted Munky in Paul Specht's book *Ibanez: The Untold Story*, "I wanted the low string in a low register. Tuning down to A was about as much as I could do without the sound getting too bassy and muddy . . . because we were using distortion."

Eventually technique-oriented shredders got on the extended-range bus, including Tony MacAlpine, Stephen Carpenter of the Deftones, and Tosin Abasi from Animals as Leaders. As MacAlpine told the author, "I play Ibanez RG six-, seven-, and eight-string guitars, all made of basswood bodies and rosewood fingerboards with neck-through construction. These instruments play and respond very musically. Tuning-wise, the seven-string lowest string would be B and the eight-string would be F♯. Because you are using lower strings—in the case of the seven-string, a low B—you have the ability to create fuller-sounding chords, as well as extended-scale patterns. With the B string being a fourth lower than the E, there is more depth. This is taken even further with the eight-string, which has a low F♯. This is almost a full octave lower than a standard six-string and adds the dimensions of a bass guitar but combined with the functionality of a standard guitar. It's very full-sounding axe."

Another seven-string virtuoso, Jeff Loomis of Arch Enemy (and formerly, Nevermore), told Ultimate-Guitar.com, "I was initially using six-strings for the first couple of Nevermore records . . . when we decided to record *Dead Heart in a Dead World* back in 2000, I had a luthier friend of mine make me a seven string and when I first started playing it, it was just so intense-sounding. I was going into a Mesa Boogie [amplifier] with an Ibanez Tube Screamer [overdrive pedal] in front of it. I just got this brutal sound. So I decided to write that whole album with that guitar. That was kind of a turning point for Nevermore as far as sound goes. . . . That's how I came to be known as a seven-string player. . . . I ended up doing that for about 18 more years with Nevermore and the seven-string kind of became my signature instrument. I have my own signature guitar with Schecter called the Jeff Loomis JL7 model."

Once a unicorn in the guitar world, extended-range axes are now perfectly common in all veins of metal and thrash. They are so prevalent that there are even seven-string versions of such venerable solidbodies as the Gibson Les Paul and Fender Stratocaster. ⚡

BRIAN "HEAD" WELCH OF KORN LAYS DOWN SOME SEVEN-STRING DROPPED-A TONES.

END OF THE 88

As the glitzy glam metal of the 1980s rolled into the uncomfortable, brooding '90s, loud rock and roll splintered in frenetic directions. Suddenly there were not merely hard rock, metal, and thrash categories; now you could find groove metal, alt-thrash, industrial, emo-metal, the punky sounds of crossover-thrash, metalcore, goth, death metal, doom, industrial, nü-metal, and other eyebrow-raising categories. A good example of the hybridization, Faith No More scored a 1990 hit with the prog-thrash-rap anthem, "Epic."

In fact it was difficult to pigeonhole many good bands from the era. Guns N' Roses was a pummeling hard rock quintet (listen to "You Could Be Mine"), but they were not *quite* metal. Pantera and Sepultura pounded out groove metal that tiptoed around thrash without being Metallica copyists. King's X mixed molten guitar with progressive rock, but it was a sound wholly their own. Alice in Chains was mistakenly lumped in with the Seattle alt-rock mob; their moody crunch spoke more of Black Sabbath than Nirvana. Deftones, Biohazard, and Suicidal Tendencies gleefully collided thrash with hardcore punk. The rap-crunch sounds of nü-metal was championed by Limp Bizkit and Korn. The classifications may not have always made sense, but it gives a sense of how quickly the music was evolving.

Veteran acts tried to pivot to these jagged little trends, yet often failing spectacularly: Steve Vai's *Sex & Religion* (1993) and *Van Halen III* (1998) albums were both egregious misfires. Even veterans like Iron Maiden, Scorpions, and Judas Priest sounded creaky and out of touch during the pioneering, breathless reign of Pantera, Nirvana, and Alice in Chains. If you bought into the hype of MTV and the rock press, the 1990s was only about alternative rock, hip-hop, punk, and grunge. But make no mistake, metal in this era was as dark and dangerous as ever. ⚡

SLASH

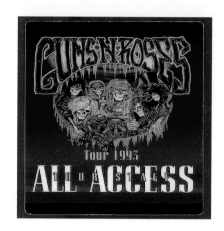

While the Reagan years delivered countless shredders—Malmsteen, Vai, Satriani, Johnson, and more—perhaps the most emblematic guitarist of the decade was a guy named Saul Hudson. Better known as Slash, he didn't emerge until 1987; but as lead guitarist for Guns N' Roses, his Les Paul 'bursts and trademark top hat became a 24/7 staple on MTV. And like Stevie Ray Vaughan—who singlehandedly resuscitated the Fender Stratocaster—Slash may have saved the Gibson Guitar Company, to the point he is now their "global brand ambassador."

On Guns N' Roses hits like "Welcome to the Jungle," "Sweet Child O' Mine," and "Paradise City," Slash (born July 23, 1965) offered an alternative to the endless tapping, whammy dives, and modal legato of '80s metalers using super-strats.

as hard as anyone, but the dressed-down look of rhythm guitarist Izzy Stradlin and intentional nods to punk hit a nerve with fans tired of glossy hair bands. Part of the album's success also came from Mike Clink's right-hook-to-the-jaw production, which avoided gloss in favor of beefy guitar, bass, and drum sounds, much like early Led Zeppelin, Sex Pistols, and Van Halen records. In the United States alone, *Appetite for Destruction* sold more than 18 million copies.

Thinking of his earliest guitar memories, Slash told Matt Wilson in *Kerrang!* magazine, "I remember that moment . . . when I first got that [Boss] mustard-yellow distortion box . . . and played [the Ted Nugent song] 'Cat Scratch Fever,' it was like a eureka moment. . . . I roughly started playing when I was 14, but I was maybe 16 when I had that amp,

doubleneck. A backline of Marshalls was essential for creating his super-saturated distortion tone, plugging into 1959T Super Lead, JCM800, and Silver Jubilee heads.

Of his Les Paul infatuation, Slash told Sweetwater's Nick Bowcott, "When I was a kid and heard *Led Zeppelin II*, I remember [hearing] "Whole Lotta Love" and "Heartbreaker" . . . and *that* sound. As I got older, I came to see it as a cool, sexy guitar; it turned out that "Whole Lotta Love" was played on a Les Paul. I always just felt very comfortable on a Les Paul, both sonically and aesthetically."

Appetite was followed by the acoustic ballad "Patience" and two-volume *Use Your Illusion* albums of 1991 with "You Could Be Mine" (heard in the blockbuster flick *Terminator 2*) and power ballad, "November Rain"—a hit so pervasive it became that generation's own "Stairway to Heaven" or "Bohemian Rhapsody." By the mid-1990s, Guns N' Roses and Metallica were the two biggest hard-rock and metal bands on Earth.

SLASH OFFERED AN ALTERNATIVE TO THE ENDLESS TAPPING, WHAMMY DIVES, AND MODAL LEGATO.

Gibson in hand, he rekindled the previous generation's use of five-note pentatonic scales, mixing melody and soul with the Lamborghini-speed blues licks of Michael Schenker, Gary Moore, and Buck Dharma. It was a wake-up call for an entire generation of guitarists.

After a slow start, the "Welcome to the Jungle" video landed a slot on MTV, at first only shown in the middle of the night—the move was a masterstroke, as insomniac viewers went berserk. Guns N' Roses rocked

guitar, [and] distortion box combo . . . Aerosmith's *Rocks* was the pivotal influence for me back then. The band's attitude and that sloppy, hard-rock thing made me go, 'Woah!'"

For gear, Slash recorded the debut record not with vintage Les Paul flametops but exact *replicas* built by luthiers Kris Derrig and Max Baranet. Once GN'R started touring and earning money, the guitarist shelled out for authentic Gibsons, as well as an EDS-1275 doubleneck and half-electric/half-acoustic Guild

Today Mr. Saul Hudson splits his time between a reunited GN'R and own solo band, plus oversees a cottage industry of signature Les Pauls, acoustics, Marshall amps, Dunlop and MXR pedals, Seymour Duncan humbuckers, and Ernie Ball strings. These are just a sampling of the guitar gear that Slash endorses, revealing the enormous pop-culture impact of his name, likeness—and yes, that sweet, fat tone. ⚡

SLASH, SANS TOP HAT, ROCKS HIS KRIS DERRIG REPLICA LES PAUL IN 1988.

⚡ ZAKK WYLDE

Zakk Wylde is one of the *last* of the old-school guitar heroes, full of rockstar swagger and unrepentant licks. In a long tenure with metal icon Ozzy Osbourne, Wylde cut a muscular figure, delivering a full range of riffage, from vintage Black Sabbath to contemporary drop-D crunch, while on hits like "Mama, I'm Coming Home," crisp acoustic playing emerged. Wylde also leads Black Label Society and his tongue-in-cheek cover act, Zakk Sabbath. He's a socialmedia star too: A YouTube video of the guitarist playing Black Sabbath's "N.I.B."—on a tiny Hello Kitty acoustic—has gleaned 15 million views.

Coming from the hinterlands of southern New Jersey, Wylde (born January 14, 1967) landed that most prestigious of gigs, the guitar slot in Ozzy's group in 1988, launching the most commercially successful era of the singer's career. In short order the

tion of players. In fact Wylde's "Guitar Solo" on Ozzy's *Live & Loud* (1993) is almost a direct homage to Marino. He told Nick Bowcott of Sweetwater, "If you listen to [Frank Marino's] feel, his technique—it's all there. Just give him a twelve-bar chord progression and he'll destroy it. He's one of my top three [influences]."

There are also the Southern sounds he courted on his 1994 *Pride & Glory* album. Wylde told the author, "People always ask me if I was always into Southern rock when I was a kid, but really, I was a total Black Sabbath freak. All my buddies were into Lynyrd Skynyrd and the Allman Brothers Band, but I was Sabbath all the way. Then when I ended up with Ozzy—which was a weird coincidence anyway—I didn't want to listen to Sabbath all the time, since I heard the guy singing every night. So [for the *Pride & Glory* album] I started

graphics. For a recent Black Label Society album, he said, "I used my 'bullseye' 1981 Les Paul Custom loaded with EMG humbuckers, and plugged into Marshall JCM800 2203 heads, Dunlop pedals, and even a Roland Jazz Chorus 120 amp. For 'T.A.Z.,' I used an Alvarez-Yairi acoustic. Today my new Wylde Audio guitars are made with all the classic ingredients as my original bullseye Les Paul."

Onstage, Wylde's rig is a simple setup of Marshall stacks and a few key pedals, as he has a strong aversion to the confluence of digital technology and guitar gear: "I *hate* MIDI. When I first joined Ozzy, I got conned into that whole rack and MIDI thing, but you needed something from freakin' NASA to figure it out if it ever conked out onstage. One night my rack went down at Hammersmith Odeon in London, as I was getting ready for my big guitar solo. My whole rack went out and the backup amp was busted; Ozzy just walked off the stage in disgust. Now I always play my Marshalls dry and, if I need a little more echo, I'll tell the soundman to add a little. If the amp blows up, the other is still going. A 10-year-old could run my setup." ⚡

"MY BUDDIES WERE INTO LYNYRD SKYNYRD ... BUT I WAS SABBATH ALL THE WAY."

picker played on several of Oz's highest-charting albums, including *No Rest for the Wicked* (1988), *No More Tears* (1991), and *Ozzmosis* (1995).

Deciphering Wylde's influences is reasonably straightforward, including hard-rock and metal players, as well as the fusion of Di Meola and McLaughlin. One key inspiration is Canadian speeder Frank Marino, whose 1978 live album influenced a genera-

listening to all the old Southern stuff because it made me feel like was at home with my buds again. Then I totally OD'd on Southern rock: Skynyrd, Allmans, Outlaws, Marshall Tucker Band, just all of 'em."

For gear, the guitar flash is best known for his bullseye Gibson Les Paul Custom, as well as his own line of Wylde Audio solidbodies, many bearing the bullseye or other custom

⚡ DIMEBAG DARRELL

At an April 10, 1992, gig at the Philadelphia Spectrum, opening act Pantera delivered a blitzkrieg set while a mosh pit roiled out front, bodies flying through the air and Dimebag Darrell's guitar scorching the 18,000-seat arena. After the set, as headliners Skid Row prepared to hit the stage, half the audience simply got up and left. It was an apt metaphor for early-'90s rock, confirming that the hair-metal fad was over.

The Age of Pantera had arrived.

Following their major label debut, *Cowboys from Hell*, Pantera set about creating the all-important followup. Two major events shaped the creation of 1991's *Vulgar Display of Power*. The first was the arrival of Metallica's smash "black album," perceived by some as a betrayal of their thrash roots, but it gave Pantera the idea to record the heaviest record of all time.

young band that could really do the business. We were in the middle of *Vulgar Display*, working real hard and not wanting to break our concentration, but we got the call asking us with play Metallica and AC/DC, and we couldn't pass that up. The show went great; even though Russian fans can't speak English, they could still feel the emotion in our music."

Despite his metal virtuosity, Dimebag was a humble young man. Even his analysis of his own playing was self-effacing: "I don't have great chops—and I don't *want* any. I play more of the legato Van Halen stuff than you think and my left hand is doing most of the work. . . . Being from Texas figures into my playing because there's a lot of great players down there, like Bugs Henderson, Jimmy Wallis, and Ricky Lynn. You hear a lot about Austin players, but

comes from my Randall stacks," he explained. "At first, it sounded like a chainsaw and I bet myself that someday I could make it my own. After a year and a half, I found it. The funny thing is they're solid-state amps, but everybody thinks they're tube, and I use six RG100HTs onstage now. I don't have a pedalboard that's thirty feet long—just a Furman PQ4 parametric EQ and blue MXR six-band EQ for my tone."

A Washburn endorser after 1994's *Far Beyond Driven*, Dimebag made his name playing classic Dean solidbodies. "For guitars, I used Deans, because to me, they're fighting weapons! I search for old ones all the time, especially the ML models, which is half-Flying V, half-Explorer with the huge headstock and 22 frets. I put Floyd Rose whammies on 'em and install Bill Lawrence L500L or L500XL pickups. Also, I'm not a dude who's getting a brand-new Boogie or Soldano amp shipped to him every week—that's why so many guitarists don't have their own sound." ⚡

"I'VE ALWAYS WANTED MY OWN TONE AND A LOT OF IT COMES FROM MY RANDALL STACKS."

While recording at Pantego Sound—the Texas studio owned by Darrell and brother Vinnie's father—the band got a call to play the Monsters of Rock festival in Moscow, Russia, in front of *500,000* metalheads.

As Dimebag (born Darrell Abbott, 1966) told the author in '92, a dozen years before his tragic onstage murder, "They needed one more band to fill the show and this Russian promoter said he wanted a

all my favorites are from Dallas. For rockers, I was inspired big-time by *Van Halen* and *Van Halen II*. Randy Rhoads, Michael Schenker, and especially Ace Frehley were important, too. I listen to Eddie before I go onstage, to get some of the spontaneity and liveliness of his playing."

As for the gear, Darrell's choices were based on a solid, but unusual sonic philosophy. "I've always wanted my own tone and a lot of it

DIMEBAG DARRELL IN 1994 WITH HIS MOST RECOGNIZABLE ML MODEL DEAN SOLIDBODY.

TY TABOR

Is King's X a metal band? A progressive band? Pearl Jam bassist Jeff Ament once told MTV, "King's X invented grunge!" Perhaps all are true, as this Houston-based outfit is one of rock's most eclectic outfits. While they've been touring for decades, fame has *infamously* eluded them—the trio is the living definition of "cult band."

With strong press support, King's X delivered an early knockout with 1989's *Gretchen Goes to Nebraska*, finding a sweet-spot between Beatlesque grandeur, Led Zep mysticism, and heavy groove-dom. A key facet was the drop-D tuning of guitarist Ty Tabor (born September 17, 1961) and lefty bassist dUg [as he formats his first name now] Pinnick, heard in "Out of a Silent Planet" and the shoulda-been-a-big-hit "Summerland." With Pinnick's larynx-shredding vocals, the latter track also

it can be heard, but we don't depend on the effect to make the track work. My guitars, in comparison, are completely dry and there's no echo at all. I just turn volume down on the guitar to get a clean tone, and up to get distortion."

Tabor kept his tone a closely guarded secret until the author deduced what kind of amplifier in a 1991 article for *Guitar for the Practicing Musician* magazine, writing that that Ty's amp was, ". . . a quasi-Gibson unit whose model he won't divulge (though judging by his tone, some kind of Lab Series head seems a solid guess)." As it turned out, the unit was indeed a solid-state Lab Series L5 preamp, routed into a separate power amp and cabinets.

For guitars, Tabor is something of an omnivore, using Strats, Yamaha super-strats, Gibson Les Pauls, and six-strings from Hamer and Zion.

Riding a wave of critical acclaim, 1990's *Faith Hope Love* positioned King's X to break to a larger audience, thanks to sumptuous hard rock like "It's Love," as radio-ready an anthem as anything from that era. Its finale was a wild jam echoing Cream's "Badge," providing a perfect setup for extended Tabor soloing—yet the album stalled at #85 on the Billboard 200 album chart. Four years later found the trio playing live for a vast cable-TV audience at the Woodstock '94 festival, including a cover of Jimi Hendrix's "Manic Depression." At the same time, their grunge-tinged single "Dogman" was in heavy radio rotation on MTV. Still, they were frustrated by weak chart performance.

THE ESSENTIAL TABOR WALL-OF-GUITAR TONE IS BIG, FAT, AND SUPERDRY.

sported Tabor's clean arpeggios and melodic solos—his tasty playing was a notch above '80s shredding.

The essential Ty Tabor *wall-of-guitar* tone is big, fat, and superdry. With broad influences—ranging from Alex Lifeson and Brian May to Ace Frehley and Christian virtuoso Phil Keaggy—his playing was just as complex. Tabor said, "King's X uses a lot of effects, but we don't drown our songs out. We use them to help put something in its own space where

There was a Guilford Ty Tabor signature model, but his most notable plank is a very specific Fender. He said, "I use those old, early 1980s Stratocaster Elite series. The pickups are kind of noisy, but they have coolest single-coil sound I've ever heard. I generally use all the pickups on the guitar, but mostly just the bridge." The active-electronic Elites also contained a TBX treble/bass expander circuit and a midrange booster with 12dB of gain.

Despite plenty of industry muscle, musicianship, and ear-grabbing songs, King's X never won over the fickle rock–and-roll audience and thus doomed to the dreaded *cult* label. Fortunately their mantle as "influencers" remains inarguable—dozens of bands point to the threesome's drop-D tuning and progressive metal as revolutionary rock of the Bush and Clinton years. ⚡

TY TABOR OF KING'S X IS SOMETHING OF AN OMNIVORE, USING STRATS, YAMAHA SUPER-STRATS, AND SIX-STRINGS FROM HAMER AND ZION.

JERRY CANTRELL

With breakout albums during the first half of the 1990s, Alice in Chains was tagged as a grunge pioneer; and they *were*—but certainly much more. The quartet exploded out of Seattle almost parallel to Nirvana, sharing a similarly brooding approach, yet of the two, AiC was a defiantly proud metal act. The sound crystalized on FM explosions like "Man in a Box," "Rooster," and "Would" that reflected the doom of vintage Sabbath yet was updated for a modern audience weaned on Metallica and Slayer. Another important point was that guitarist Jerry Cantrell, unlike so many grungers, actually played big, hairy solos.

The essential sound of Alice in Chains combined the pounding grooves of Cantrell—their chief songwriter—with the harrowing, powerhouse vocals of Layne Staley, often centered on lyrics about ad-

acted and sang in the high-school choir, which helped shape the future sound of their vocal harmonies. His early guitar influences include Eddie Van Halen and Tony Iommi of Black Sabbath, telling Sean Allen at IGN, "I'm not a very schooled guitar player [and] learned to play by ear . . . emulating my heroes until I found my own sound. As far as technically knowing what scale I'm playing, I'm not really that great at it."

It's important to note that Alice in Chains' debut album, *Facelift*, came out in 1990—a year before the grunge explosion. Their uptempo "We Die Young" already exhibited the dropped-D riffing that became a hallmark of the genre, while the hit "Man in a Box" found Cantrell using a talkbox effects unit to heighten his distortion tone. Talking to Nick Bowcott of Sweetwater, the AiC guitarist said, "Van Halen or Sab-

the grunge tag prevailed. Cantrell's soulful, warm-toned distortion solo in "Would" was a refreshing break from years of overwrought shred guitar, while his power chords were in the '90s sweet spot mined by Nirvana, Stone Temple Pilots, and Soundgarden. Cantrell's verse to "Them Bones" featured a radical chromatic riff that scored high points for originality and excitement. Conversely Alice in Chains released several EPs focusing on acoustic guitar, like *Sap* and *Jar of Flies* from 1994, as well as played a hit *MTV Unplugged* concert.

For over 30 years, Cantrell has been associated with G&L guitars, particularly the Rampage he's long favored. He told Sweetwater that his circa-1984 Rampage was based on Eddie Van Halen's famed "Frankenstein" axe, loaded with one pickup and one volume knob. Today, G&L carries several signature Jerry Cantrell Rampage and Superhawk models. ⚡

UNLIKE SO MANY GRUNGERS, CANTRELL ACTUALLY PLAYED BIG, HAIRY SOLOS.

diction and substance abuse (which claimed the singer's life in 2002). Also critical to the formula were tight vocal harmonies from Staley and Cantrell, which added a dimension lost on most other grunge-era acts—as well as brilliant engineering and co-production from Dave Jerden.

A largely self-taught player, young Cantrell (born March 18, 1966)

bath is probably where I picked up on the dropped-D thing. Yeah, I think 'Unchained' or like a Sabbath riff or something . . . but 'Unchained' has got that sick riff with the flanger on that. . . . I always liked that darker kind of sound."

From 1992, the multiplatinum *Dirt* album turned Alice in Chains into a top sludge-metal act, though again,

TOM MORELLO

Tom Morello is not only a grunge star and notable 1990s guitarist but also a political activist, co-leader of mega-bands like Rage Against the Machine and Audioslave, and occasional sideman to Bruce Springsteen. RATM carved out its niche with a brand of *groove* rock—part grunge, part hip-hop, and part thrash and punk guitar. As a six-stringer, Morello subverted the noise innovations of Adrian Belew and Sonic Youth into a controlled rhythmic fury, dropping big riffs infused with "solos" laden with Digitech Whammy Pedal squeals and drum-like "killswitch" patterns. It instantly made the guitarist stand out from the alt-rock pack.

Morello (born May 30, 1964) grew up listening to a wide variety of music, from Public Enemy and Run-DMC to The Clash, Bob Dylan, Woody Guthrie, Led Zeppelin, and fusion guitar wizard Allan Holdsworth. Heard

Woodstock 1999 to see how concert-goers react feverishly to the band's ass-shaking grooves.

Wearing his guitar up high, more like a country guitarist, Morello locks into the beat and deploys a strangely simple rig—something he feels strongly about. As he told Red Bull TV's *Gearheads* show, "My take on gear is that it does not matter at all, *ever*, in any circumstance. . . . Creating music with whatever wires and piece of wood you have, that's a creative and an intellectual and an emotional exercise. . . . People are all [asking me], 'What [kind of] strings do you use?' It couldn't matter less! . . . I'm not going to worry about gear anymore . . . I was chasing this elusive tone and finally, one day, I gave up. I spent a couple of hours at rehearsal [and] marked the settings on my amp . . . I got it as good as I could, [and] I finally stopped tinker-

the original plank. Other guitars in his arsenal include a Fender Aerodyne Soul Power Stratocaster and 1980s Telecaster with a "Sendero Luminoso" sticker, most used for dropped-D parts. His rig has long been a Marshall JCM800 2205 50-watt head, Peavey 4 x 12 cabinet, and a variety of stompboxes, including his ubiquitous Digitech Whammy Pedal, name famous on RATM's "Killing in the Name."

Morello's gear philosophy jives with his overall feelings about making music and using his guitar to deliver a social message rather than showing off chops. He told *Concertlivewire.com*, "I don't think that it requires walls of Marshall stacks or Les Paul guitars to make music that is heavy and impactful. Compare, for example, Bob Dylan's 'A Hard Rain's A-Gonna Fall' with any number of noisy, pointless emo bands. Sometimes when the volume is turned down, the heaviness is amplified." ⚡

MORELLO LOCKS INTO THE BEAT AND DEPLOYS A STRANGELY SIMPLE RIG.

on tracks like "Killing in the Name" and "Bulls on Parade," his heavily distorted riffs are as molten as Tony Iommi or James Hetfield's, but laden with hip-hop syncopation. The quartet's music was almost scientifically designed to make *thousands* of people jump, leap, dance, and mosh at a Rage Against the Machine live show. Witness clips of their performance at

ing with the Frankenstein guitar that I have. This is the tone that I have . . . what are the songs that I'm going to make with this?"

True to those concepts, Morello uses a minimal number of guitars, including his nameless "Arm the Homeless" super-strat—one he's played for decades and modified so heavily that only the body remains of

KIM THAYIL

For evidence that Black Sabbath had *deep* roots inside the grunge movement, look no further than Soundgarden. Somehow this Seattle foursome played slow rock that was unquestionably alternative and modern sounding—yet the sludge crunch of guitarist Kim Thayil, bassist Ben Shepherd, and drummer Matt Cameron was just as clearly old-school stoner rock. On top of it all, vocalist/guitarist Chris Cornell bucked the baritone range of many grunge singers and delivered a tenor blast more akin to Robert Plant and Ozzy Osbourne than Kurt Cobain. All these ingredients made Soundgarden one of the most interesting bands of the era.

The band was formed as early 1984, but it took until 1991's *Badmotorfinger* and the blockbuster *Superunknown* (1994) to make Soundgarden a household word. Tracks like

For gear, Kim Thayil's weapon of choice was an unusual Guild S-100, which is a thicker-body variant of Gibson's iconic SG, while the singer riffed on Les Paul Customs and, later, an olive-green Chris Cornell ES-335 from the Gibson Custom Shop. By the time of 1996's *Down on the Upside*, Thayil was experimenting with more gear, as he told Rich Maloof in *Guitar* magazine: "I used a lot of different amps, a lot of different guitars. On *Louder Than Love* and *Badmotorfinger*, I used a lot of humbucking. On this album, I used the Guild S-100 quite a bit, but I used a lot of Telecaster and Jazzmaster as well. And there is more acoustic guitar on this record, plus dobro, mandolas, and the occasional keyboard—but it's never overdone; it's just there for color."

For the remainder of the Soundgarden guitarist's prime-era rig,

Ibanez chorus, and Mu-tron phase shifter ("Applebite"). Thayil prefers Dunlop .73 mm picks and Ernie Ball Super Slinky strings, with heavier bass strings for drop tunings."

Ironically, despite the strong Sabbath vibe in Soundgarden's grunge, Thayil outright rejects that notion. As he further told Rich Maloof in *Guitar* magazine, "Yeah, we weren't influenced by Led Zeppelin and Black Sabbath. The past few days in interviews we've been asked that. We said, 'Look, if anything, *you* drew a parallel.' If they say that we sounded like those bands, we'd say okay, and I might be able to accept that. But if you say that we drew from their body of work and created what we do out of that, it's like, 'No, that was never the case.' When I started playing guitar, I was listening to Johnny Ramone [and] MC5. There may have been things we've done in the past that sounded similar, but that certainly wasn't because of influences. It was probably happenstance."

"WHEN I STARTED PLAYING, I WAS LISTENING TO JOHNNY RAMONE [AND] MC5."

"Outshined" and "Rusty Cage" exuded equal parts Sabbath, King's X, and hardcore punk, inciting fans at 1992's traveling Lollapalooza festival. Their single "Black Hole Sun" distilled the best of Soundgarden's heaviness into a radio-ready anthem, creating a psychedelic MTV smash—thanks in part to Cornell's star-turning vocal and Thayil's sickly modulated arpeggios. It also opened the door to more hits, like "Fell on Black Days."

Wolf Marshall wrote in *Vintage Guitar Magazine*, "Thayil has played a number of amps. An early favorite was the Peavey VTM-120. By the mid '90s, he favored Mesa Boogie Dual Rectifiers with 4 x 12 cabs for solos, and 50-watt Mavericks for rhythm. He supplemented his rig with Fender Super, Princeton, Twin Reverb and Vibro-King combos, along with a vintage Orange head. . . . His effects included a Dunlop Rotovibe, wah,

INDUSTRIAL STRENGTH

While 1990s FM rock was seemingly dominated by grunge, alt-rock, and the reemergence of punk (think Green Day, Rancid, and The Offspring), there were other sounds that that decade—and few as bone-crushing as industrial rock, also known as alternative metal. This subgenre was marked by droning, high-saturation guitars, massive beats, lo-fi production, and eternally bleak lyrics, exemplified by Nine Inch Nails, Type O Negative, Tool, Ministry, Godflesh, Pitchshifter, and a host of gloomy metalurgists.

Among them, Tool was the perfectly named industrial band, as guitarist Adam Jones dropped his compressed crunch onto "Sober" and "Schism" using a silverburst 1979 Les Paul Custom. As he told the Dutch television show *Onrust!* about why he loves his '79 Gibson, he said, "It's the control of the highs and the lows . . . the sustain [of] the notes and how long you can hold it. . . . When it gets electric, it's just a complete different world." Jones takes a dim view, however, of the term *heavy metal*, noting, "I really don't like glam metal. When people call [Tool] metal, . . . I feel like taking a bath because, to me, metal is kind of embarrassing."

Another fierce act was Ministry, led by frontman Al Jourgensen (who sometimes played a coffin-shaped Schecter solidbody), but notably positioning the late Mike Scaccia as lead guitarist. Listen to the thrashy "Psalm 69" for evidence of his high-speed Les Paul ripping. Scaccia died onstage with the band Rigor Mortis in 2012, later eulogized by ex-Pantera singer Philip Anselmo: "I have traveled the world playing music, and I've been fortunate to play with extremely talented guitarists. . . . But when it came down to extremities, I've known since 1987 who the fastest, most precise player on this planet was, and that was the one and only Mike Scaccia. The playing field is now even."

A critic's darling, Helmet was a New York quartet led by guitarist Page Hamilton—a player known for using deep, dark tunings—and hip with the artsy, noise-rock crowd. As he told writer Baker Rorick in 1994, "I do one song with an early '80s G&L SC-2 that's dropped down to A. The bottom four strings are down as close to A as you can get, and then I tune the top two to C♯ and G, so it's A7 chord on top. Everyone asks, 'What processing is on the guitar?' And I reply, 'What processing? It's just guitar—going straight into an amp.' God, it sounds sweet."

One of the biggest metal hits of the day was Danzig's "Mother," with John Christ in charge of the menacing riffage. Describing his gear, he told *Guitar Shop* magazine that ". . . the B. C. Rich has a real warm, fat, round bottom-end that's great for chunkin'. Chords are really full-sounding. I have three Biches, including one that used to be a 10-string." His amps in the Danzig era were Marshalls, plus a VHT Pitbull. Christ added, "I've been hitting the front of the VHT with a distortion unit for solos. I've been playing around with the Boss DS-1 and Turbo Overdrive—and I don't know too many players who don't have a GE-7 graphic EQ in their rig."

Lastly White Zombie was known for its singular brand of horror-movie metal, based on the stage antics of frontman Rob Zombie and guitarist Jay Yuenger, known for playing angular Ibanez Iceman axes. The latter told *Machinemusic. net*, "When people first heard [White Zombie], they were mystified by it because they couldn't tell whether it was metal or not. The simple answer to that is, 'It's metal, but it's also other things. Why is that challenging to you?' It's normal now, but then it was not. . . . You can hear it very clearly on *La Sexorcisto*, we're obviously very into Slayer. . . . We're very into hip hop. . . . You have to remember that this [was] New York City in 1991 or 1990 . . . [we were] at the right place in the right time." ⚡

TOP: ADAM JONES OF TOOL AND HIS SILVERBURST ONSTAGE IN COPENHAGEN, DENMARK, 2019.
BOTTOM LEFT: PAGE HAMILTON OF CRITICS' FAVORITES HELMET.
BOTTOM RIGHT: JAY YUENGER OF WHITE ZOMBIE POSES WITH ONE OF HIS IBANEZ ICEMAN AXES.

As the twentieth century wound down, the amount of volcanic met-al spewing into the atmosphere was overwhelming. There were now *thousands* of bands, many with cult followings and small-label record deals—enough for fans to provide all-important support. Beyond the general category of "heavy metal," there were now micro-subgenres for melodic death metal, grindcore, crust punk, Scandinavian black metal, groove metal, extreme metal, math metal, symphonic metal, power metal, and more. It became dizzying.

This late-century approach drew inspiration from big names like Black Sabbath, Judas Priest, Iron Maiden, Metallica, and Pantera but also lesser-known influencers like Napalm Death, Carcass, Death, Mercyful Fate, Morbid Angel, and Emperor. Once mortal enemies, met-al and punk started to cross-pollinate regularly, thanks to the innova-tions of Motörhead and Killing Joke. One can't diminish the impact of slasher movies and gory computer games—at times, death-metal and grindcore bands seemed to be the rock equivalent of the Oscar-win-ning horror film *The Silence of the Lambs*, or Playstation video game *Resident Evil*.

Musically few of the new metal bands exuded much in the way of melody—rhythm was king, as it promoted the brutal herd mentality that concertgoers craved. The violent bonding rituals of the mosh pit were dominant, despite the potential for physical injury. Lastly crunchy guitars, bass, and incessant double-kick drums ruled the sonosphere, leaving room for a frontman's guttural "death growl" vocals.

Once feared as a symptom of social and moral decay, modern met-al—and its rapidly mutating offspring—had seeped into every crack and crevice on Earth. ⚡

DEATH METAL

When the first death metal bands arrived in the late 1980s and throughout the '90s, it felt like a line had been crossed. Beyond the thrashy riffs and hyperspeed grooves, the genre's lyrics were straight out of the most grotesque slasher movies, exemplified by titles on the first Death album: "Mutilation," "Regurgitated Guts," and "Torn to Pieces" among them. Key bands were aptly named Obituary, Napalm Death, Autopsy, and Deicide. No subject was off-limits—the grimmer and grosser, the better. Fans loved it.

Hailing from Altamonte Springs, Florida, the quartet Death is considered, appropriately enough, the first death-metal band; and their 1987 *Scream Bloody Gore* remains a masterpiece of the genre. "Denial of Life" and "Infernal Death" all speak to the thud of Metallica and Slayer—the latter's pivotal *Reign in Blood* album

had come out the previous year and was a key influence. On guitar, bass, and vocals, leader Chuck Schuldiner (1967–2001) devised brutal, careening riffs and dropped skittering shred solos all over the place. For gear, he used a pointy B. C. Rich Stealth through a Marshall Valvestate 8100 solid-state amp, set with seriously reduced midrange levels—a sound popularly known as "scooped mids."

Schuldiner passed away from brain cancer in 2001, and today, he's renowned as the father of death metal. As for his original intentions in creating the band Death, he once told Mark Morton at Examiner.com that he wanted, ". . . to play some of the heaviest metal that hopefully there could ever be; to always get better at what we were doing. And for myself as a guitar player, I've always wanted to get better but stay true to the music—never wimp out or whip out any power ballads."

Carcass is another leader of the movement, though variously labeled as death, grindcore (a punk/metal

BILL STEER OF BRITISH DEATH METALERS CARCASS.

hybrid), goregrind, and even melodic death. Fronted by guitar ace Bill Steer (born December 3, 1969), the British band blended guttural vocals with advanced musicianship—their playing was as tight as just about any progressive group, with Steer's virtuosic lead work leading the way. His relentless riffing, melodic harmony lines, and blitzkrieg solos on 1993's "No Love Lost" and "Heartwork" are the stuff of metal lore.

Many fans, however, may be surprised at one of Steer's biggest guitar influences. He told the blog Listen to Heavy Metal, "[Irish blues-rock guitarist] Rory Gallagher was one of the reasons I started playing guitar. He was a big influence on me. . . . Very early on, when I [was] first getting into rock music I saw him on TV. . . . Not only could he play and sing well, but [Gallagher] seemed really humble and down to earth . . . that had a lot to do with me pursuing electric guitar as a young kid."

Morbid Angel guitarist Trey Azagthoth (born March 26, 1965) was heavier than hell, proven on "God of Emptiness," a slow, morose elegy once featured on MTV's Beavis & Butt-Head cartoon. "Rapture," from 1993's Covenant, sounded like Metallica trapped in heavy sludge, at least until Azagthoth's supershred break, typically on a B. C. Rich Ironbird solidbody. The band also tunes down

to D♯, which the guitarist says delivers a different vibe than standard tuning, as he told Disposable Underground: "Everything has got a little frequency to it. Everything is moving, all the molecules are moving . . . I can't explain any better than that. I like chopping [on] a D♯ or whatever it is, better than an E. It had a more evil feel."

A cousin to death metal, the sounds of doom rock and stoner metal also grew in popularity throughout the 1990s, as fans rediscovered the power and glory of early Black Sabbath. Critical bands were the Grammy-winning High on Fire and Sleep—both bands featuring guitarist Matt Pike—as well as Electric Wizard, and Sunn O))).

Perhaps doom's best-known band was Kyuss with guitarist Josh Homme (born May 17, 1973), who also went on to chart success with Queens of the Stone Age, Eagles of Death Metal, and Them Crooked Vultures (featuring ex-Led Zeppelin bassist John Paul Jones and Foo Fighters' Dave Grohl). From 1994, Kyuss's "Gardenia" sounded like a secret, unreleased cut from Sabbath's *Vol. 4*—full of punky, lo-fi fuzz and vengeful fury. Homme's tar-like riffing makes for a sublime example of stoner/doom rock.

BLACK METAL

If there's a detonation point for this powerful subgenre, 1982's *Black Metal* by Venom is an apt starting point. Led by Venom, Bathory, Mercyful Fate, and Hellhammer, the name "black metal" refers to Satanic, often anti-Christian themes in the lyrics, while its music merged NWOBHM, thrash, and punk with freakish abandon. There were groups emerging all over Europe, but Norway and the Scandinavian countries became its epicenter, forging a mental image of cold, brutal rock—as if played by godless Vikings.

Switzerland's Celtic Frost was an extreme black-metal act, releasing *To Mega Therion* as early as 1985 and influencing endless bands—surprisingly, even Nirvana. With guitarist, singer, and songwriter Tom G. Warrior (born July 19, 1963), Celtic Frost's crunch was a shock to the system, deploying slow, grinding tempos and atonal chord riffs, and avoiding clichés, heard in "The Usurper" and "Circle of the Tyrants." Wielding an Ibanez Iceman, Warrior later played with vicious acts like Hellhammer and Triptykon, but to many metalheads, he'll forever be known as the mastermind behind Celtic Frost.

Cradle of Filth is another act that tiptoes between black and extreme categories, plus symphonic touches, earning global acclaim. Their 1994 *The Principle of Evil Made Flesh* album put the British band on the map and featured lead guitarist Paul Allender, who was an on-again/off-again member over the decades. Allender was a devotee of PRS solidbodies, plugged into a Mesa/Boogie amp.

Somewhere in between black metal, death, and prog rock lies Opeth, a huge band from Sweden fronted by vocalist/guitarist Mikael Åkerfeldt. Their 1994 album *Orchid* captured that uncanny mix of Scandinavian and progressive sounds, featuring the six-strings of Åkerfeldt and Peter Lindgren, both of whom favor PRS models. Of Opeth's unique approach, Åkerfeldt told Metal Injection: "I don't think it's traditional heaviness, like when you talk about heavy and metal music. I kind of reevaluated what I think is heavy in the last couple of years . . . turning up the distortion and tuning down . . . doesn't make it heavy to me anymore. . . . So, we went the other way. We never tuned down. . . . Some of those parts that are slow and doomy just sound heavier."

MASKS & MAKEUP

Thanks to rockers like Alice Cooper and Kiss (and even earlier, The Crazy World of Arthur Brown), there have been generations of kids who grew up wanting to play in a loud band—and wear makeup onstage. The idea certainly owes a debt to circuses and carnivals, where entertainers disguise themselves in order to create an otherworldly, vaguely sinister atmosphere. Yet by the millennium, metalheads had definitively brought that stage magic to the concert arena, mixing violent riffs and ritualistic face paint to the delight of headbangers everywhere.

As a solo artist, and frontman with Mercyful Fate, the rocker known as King Diamond shrouds himself in demonic paint—and hits the stage holding a microphone mounted on a cross of faux human bones. For forty years,

he's delivered a crafty of commercial hard rock and black metal, with nods to the pop-horror accessibility of Ozzy Osbourne (fellow metalers Rob Zombie and now-canceled Marilyn Manson also updated Ozzy's stagemanship to modern specs). The Norwegian black-metal band Gorgoroth is known for their own brand of zombie makeup, brutal rhythms—and guitarists with names like Infernus and Tormentor. Wes Borland, guitarist for the nü-metal favorite Limp Bizkit, wears a variety of masks and makeup onstage to complement his Jackson King V axes.

For mask-wearing bands, Slipknot has perhaps sold the most albums and concert tickets, blending drop-tuned thrashiness with radio-friendly, emo-inflected choruses. In fact their video for "Psychosocial" has been viewed more than 400 million times, exposing Jim Root's high-speed shred chops and Fender Flathead Telecaster (with EMG humbuckers) to the entire metal kingdom. He also has his own line of Fender Jim Root signature solidbodies, including Strat, Tele, and Jazzmaster editions.

ABOVE: TOM G. WARRIOR OF SWISS BLACK METAL ACT CELTIC FROST.
RIGHT: SLIPKNOT GUITARIST—AND FENDER SIGNATURE ARTIST—JIM ROOT.

In the pantheon of mask-wearing metalers, though, it's hard to beat the cartoonish charm of GWAR. Dressing like monsters from the Power Rangers or even Teenage Mutant Ninja Turtles kids' TV shows, its members forge a likable punk-metal hybrid to go with their monster-themed stage costumes. Plus they have a fully costumed bassist named Beefcake the Mighty, adding to the circus-like vibe of this delirious act.

You can't talk about masks without mentioning the anonymous über-shredder named Buckethead (born May 13, 1969), who played with Guns N' Roses. Wearing a white kabuki mask—and either an all-white or actual KFC fried chicken bucket on his skull—Buckethead has long blown audiences away with his ridiculously fast chops and bizarre stage getup. It's a one-of-a-kind stage outfit.

On the dark side of the force, Dimmu Borgir is categorized as a symphonic black metal, owing to their use of dramatic keyboards and progressive textures. Face-tinted guitarists such as Silenoz, Galder, Tjodalv, and Astennu

have powered the band over the decades, with Galder wielding Jackson and ESP or LTD V-shape axes. Metal institutions such as Rammstein and Ghost are hugely successful, arena-filling superstars clad in makeup, but John 5 (born July 31, 1971) is perhaps the best-known contemporary guitar hero in the costume category. Formerly with Marilyn Manson and now handling guitar duties with Rob Zombie and, as of late 2022, Mötley Crüe (as well as releasing numerous solo albums), John 5 is an avid collector of Kiss memorabilia, which shouldn't be too surprising. Yet he's a serious Telecaster shredder, both in metal and traditional country styles, replete with excellent hybrid chicken-pickin' techniques. He's also been honored with a J5 signature Tele with Fender.

Wearing either ghostly white makeup or a black-and-white mask, John 5 told Catherine Ash of Reverb.com, "I'm a connoisseur of old vintage Telecasters, and . . . I have hundreds of Telecasters . . . and the Fender Telecaster has such a great history. That guitar is meant as a county

FREDRIK THORDENDAL OF SWEDISH MATH METAL BAND MESHUGGAH.

guitar, but these guys could really play. There were unbelievable guitar players back in the '50s and '60s, so I would watch *Hee Haw*, and they all played Telecasters. . . . [This] guitar has inspired me so much, just the history of it."

MATH METAL

Call it math metal, mathcore, or even djent, but there's a vein of heavy rock that uses wickedly complex grooves—odd-meter beats and polyrhythms—to get its furious message across. With palm-muted guitar chunks, often in drop-tuning, the music gets its name for the band members' ability to play in devilish meters beyond standard 4/4 and 6/8 beats (to wit, the math). As heard for example in the djent of Periphery, some of the grooves are nearly impossible for the average musician to count off, but therein lies its charm.

Meshuggah is one of the founders of this genre, particularly the hyper-rhythmic sounds of djent, which got its name from the actual sound the guitars made. The band features lead virtuoso Fredrik Thordendal (born February 11, 1970) and co-riffer Mårten Hagström (born April 27, 1971) locking into tight patterns with the thrashy bass and drums, heard on 1994's "Humiliative." It's a brutal jam, but wait for Thordendal's liquid-legato solo, which displays the overt—and surprising—influence from jazz-rock guitar hero Allan Holdsworth. He's further known for playing Ibanez seven- and eight-string instruments.

Describing the evolution of the djent style, Meshuggah's rhythm guitarist Hagström told the YouTube channel Rauta, "I think it's a misconception, that djent thing. It's our lead guitar player Fredrik being drunk back in the day, talking to one of our old-school fans, trying to explain

what type of guitar tone we were always trying to get, and he was desperately trying to say, 'We want that 'dj-,' 'dj-,' 'dj-,' 'dj-.' And that guy was, like, 'What's he saying? Is that a Swedish word? Must be. Sounds like dj-, maybe djent'? And that's where it comes from. [Our sound is] . . . heavy, experimental music. I don't care if it's progressive or not—it's heavy. Either it gets into that math-metal, djent subgenre type of thing, that's for other people to decide. [Meshuggah plays] aggressive, experimental music, and that's basically it."

Hailing from Massachusetts, Killswitch Engage mixes math, punky metalcore, and more polished sounds into a compressed, accessible sound, such as "The End of the Heartache." The band features mutton-chopped lead guitarist Adam Dutkiewicz with rhythm man Joel Stroetzel, dropping chunky riffs over complex beats and those omnipresent double-kick drums of contemporary metal.

Describing the difference between his style and Dutkiewicz's, Stroetzel told Ivan Chopik of Guitar Messenger, "On . . . 'Never Again,' the opening riff is a good example of an Adam riff—he likes to do off-time stuff and things like that, whereas 'Light in a Darkened World' would be more of an example of something I would write. It's more European metal and more straightforward. Adam tends to think outside the box a little bit more with rhythms and cool chord voicings . . . I've always been more into the thrashy stuff."

Another mathcore pioneer is the now-defunct Dillinger Escape Plan, featuring guitarist Ben Weinman (who played various ESP models). "The Running Board" from 1998 captures the band's chaotic, yet expert use of extreme up-tempo beats in metal—countered by slow, languid sections not unlike King Crimson. Of the Dillinger Escape Plan's influences, Weinman once told Jon Robertson of Bearded Gentleman Music, ". . . in the '90s there was this horrible explosion of all the bands trying to do rap metal. . . . But what we wanted to do was blend all our influences . . . it was more like this punk and heavy aggressive band that sounds different. So eventually what we started doing was listening to all these fusion and Afro-Cuban rhythms and trying to figure how to make them sound grimy and punk." ⚡

FREDRIK THORDENDAL OF SWEDISH MATH METAL BAND MESHUGGAH.

Here in the twenty-first century, heavy metal is deeply embedded in the popular firmament. Once the province of suburban arenas and smoke-filled basements, you can hear distorted, saturated guitar tones in TV commercials, walking down supermarket aisles, and even at giant sports events, where fans erupt joyously when Metallica's "Enter Sandman" blares over the PA system.

One of the most significant improvements in modern metal has been the proliferation of women guitarists and bassists. Once the ultimate boys club, the guitar universe now has room for countless female players, including players like Lzzy Hale of Halestorm, Nita Strauss, Orianthi, Nili Brosh, and Gretchen Menn of Zepparella, a Led Zeppelin tribute act. Again YouTube is the proving ground; there, one can find endless videos of women musicians from around the globe, displaying scary technique and killer grooves on guitar and bass.

While millions of global listeners adore electronic K-pop from Korea, there are metallic equivalents: Japan's female trio Babymetal takes thrashy guitar and drums, adds silly bubblegum lyrics, and earns *hundreds of millions* of YouTube views for cuts like "Gimme Chocolate!!" (currently with hundreds of millions of views). Another wildly popular act, Evanescence mixes nü-metal, emo-rock, pop ballads, gloomy goth, and Christian themes—all to the tune of millions of albums and concert tickets sold. Similarly the band Disturbed combines drop-tuned guitar riffs with soaring vocals that wouldn't be out of place on a Nickelback record.

But is any of it real metal?

This is a topic worthy of debate, but it's a question that drives so much heavy rock after the millennium. Where fans once merely argued whether Led Zeppelin was metal or not, today there are so many variants that it's a self-perpetuating battle. Either the days of classic metal are gone—or the genre requires a *much* bigger tent. ⚡

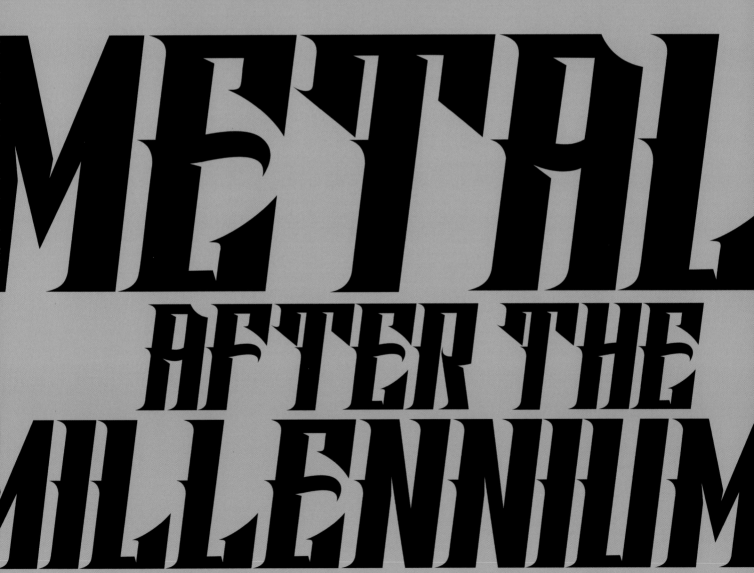

METAL AFTER THE MILLENNIUM

MARK TREMONTI

Breaking out in the late 1990s and enjoying a massive platinum run, Creed was a band that critics hated—and fans adored. Like Nickelback, Creed possessed melodic accessibility for radio and MTV but also grungy power chords for the hard-rock crowd. This combination of metal and melody has a long, bankable history (think Journey, Styx, Night Ranger, Whitesnake), but Creed took it into the alt-rock universe, thanks to the charismatic vocals of Scott Stapp and drop-D riffs of Mark Tremonti.

Over the years, Tremonti has racked up a staggering array of hit records and even a Grammy for the 2001 Creed power ballad, "With Arms Wide Open." The band's *Human Clay* album came out in 1999, and by the summer of 2000, the single "Higher" was plastered across airwaves the world over. The album was eventually certified eleven-time plat-

self-named act, Tremonti, promised more of a thrash sound but still delivered the kind of heavy melody that fans of Creed came to expect.

Tremonti (born April 18, 1974) began playing guitar at age 11 and matured into a player of staggering technical ability. Despite the commercial aspect of Creed and Alter Bridge, his chops are as fast and dexterous as any shredder out there, only adding to the allure of their brand of popular alt-metal.

Discussing his early inspirations, Tremonti told Ward Meeker of *Vintage Guitar Magazine*, "Guitar-wise, it was when I heard songs like 'Smoke on the Water,' 'Love Stinks,' and 'More Than a Feeling.' The parts where it was just guitar made me want to pick one up and play. . . . When I was young, I only really listened to the heaviest stuff I could find. . . . Early on, I used to sit

"WHEN I WAS YOUNG, I ONLY REALLY LISTENED TO THE HEAVIEST STUFF I COULD FIND."

inum. Once Creed broke up, Tremonti formed a heavier band called Alter Bridge and found another compelling vocalist, Myles Kennedy (later fronting Slash's band); the group achieved considerable success, especially in the United Kingdom. His

with Paul Gilbert's videos and learn his stuff. I also listened to a lot of Vinnie Moore . . . Satriani has always had *great* melodic sense. . . . Vai is very inventive and very cool and off-the-wall. . . . Right now, Derek Trucks is number one for me. I've

totally switched gears since I was a kid; I used to want to play as fast as possible. But now I just wanna express as much as possible. So it's Derek Trucks, Warren Hayes, Doyle Bramhall Jr., that kind of vibe."

For guitars, the musician has long played PRS models, working with the Maryland guitar company to create the Mark Tremonti signature line of single-cutaway solidbodies. Tremonti described the guitar and larger rig to Anne Erickson of Reverb.com: "To this day, one of the highlights of my career is getting that [PRS] signature guitar. It's been their top signature model since day one. It has a mahogany body and maple top and is very road-worthy and stays in tune really well. I have a signature wah pedal from Morley that I love . . . [and] use a hand-wired [Ibanez] Tube Screamer for my leads. . . . I'm not a big pedal guy. . . . I'm an amp fanatic. I collect amps like women collect purses and shoes! On tour, I use a Mesa/Boogie Dual Rectifier alongside a PRS Archon Amplifier and . . . I have Fender '65 Twin Reissues and a Bogner amp."

MARK TREMONTI WORKED WITH PRS TO CREATE A SIGNATURE LINE OF SINGLE-CUTAWAY SOLIDBODIES.

⚡ ALEXI LAIHO

The guitar universe was shattered on December 29, 2020, following the death of Alexi Laiho. A monster player known for playing melodic death metal, the Children of Bodom guitarist brought a renewed sense of Euro-metal lost during the years of grunge, alt-rock, and industrial. Echoing that six-string passion of Uli Roth, Michael Schenker, and his hero Randy Rhoads, Laiho laced his technique with neoclassical arpeggios, taps, sweeps, fast blues scales, and soaring bends. Yet this well-loved metal artist—known as "Allu" and "Wildchild" by CoB fans—was suddenly gone at age 41.

With his trademark ESP axes and black fingernails, Laiho (born April 8, 1979) led Children of Bodom to head-banging triumph for over twenty-five years, touring incessantly and building a huge following. Remembering an early gig when Laiho and

For influences the Finnish guitarman soaked up metal and even punk guitar styles of the 1970s–1990s, recalling the first album he purchased to Mark Cowles of *Performer* magazine: "So many bands come to mind, but as far as guitar playing goes, I remember the first time I heard Steve Vai's *Passion and Warfare*," remembered Laiho. "Well, I mean I was already obsessed with the guitar at that time, but when I heard that damn thing, I was like, 'I'm going to have to learn to play the guitar!' I'm still working on it [*laughs*]. . . . As far as punk goes, Sex Pistols, Misfits, The Ramones, The Exploited, stuff like that. I like the old-school stuff [from the] late '70s and early '80s."

As heard in 2013's pummeling "Halo of Blood" (from the album of the same name), Laiho dropped relentless power riffing and a terrifying solo of speed and finesse.

Starting around 2003 Alexi Laiho switched to an ESP V-style guitar—this later morphed into an extensive line of signature ESP and LTD Alexi Katakana models. Each has an offset-V design reminiscent of the Jackson Rhoads, sporting 24 extra-jumbo frets, a single humbucker (sometimes adding a neck single-coil pickup), Floyd Rose locking whammy, and sawtooth fingerboard inlays. Of his favorite ESP axes, Laiho told *Total Guitar*, "This one [has] one pickup because that's all I need. I like that mean, treble sound. It's actually a passive pickup, an EMG HZ, and I [have] a gain-boost built inside the guitar, right here with the battery and stuff. The output is actually four times stronger than an active pickup. And I got a Floyd Rose and 24 frets . . . the last three are scalloped . . . it just rings better when you do bends . . . . Looks badass, right? . . . But that's how it should be. . . . [The ESP has] the '80s look—to me, it's cool." ⚡

THE FINNISH GUITARMAN SOAKED UP METAL AND EVEN PUNK STYLES.

CoB opened for the black-metal act Dimmu Borgir, guitarist Silenoz told Loudersound.com, "We could hear the opening band playing from backstage. We were like, 'Holy sh*t, what is this?' It sounded like Yngwie Malmsteen on speed. We ran out and watched the spectacle and stood there with our jaws open."

Much like the early recordings of In Flames, you can hear the rich melodicism in Children of Bodom's "Waste of Skin," matching high-speed death metal with stacked guitar-and-keyboard harmonies and a skittering, neoclassical guitar solo that spoke to the influence of Randy Rhoads.

HERMAN LI

You can't call Herman Li another cookie-cutter speed demon. His technique is formidable, blending picking agility with ungodly tap and sweep moves—yet the DragonForce guitarist can also slow it down and play a beautiful, melodic lead. The guitarist is also a master of strange guitar noises and sounds, many derived from the beloved video games of his youth, such as Pac-Man. All of this makes the Hong Kong(China)–born British player one of the most intriguing and respected metalers of the modern era, evident on power-metal albums like *Inhuman Rampage* and *Ultra Beatdown*.

Recalling how he forged his unique guitar style, Li (born 1976) developing a simple approach to the guitar to understanding complex, progressive styles. Whammy bar techniques seemed to be a lost art for many years, and it's one of my favorite things you can do with the electric guitar. Because I was really into video games as a kid, I started relating them to those sounds and gave them video-game names. They are not too hard to do once you work out the muting techniques—and how to control the string noise."

A quintessential Dragon-Force cut is "Through the Fire and Flames," where Li drops in videogame effects with abandon. This manic tempo cut is a technical tour de force, with the guitarist splitting

ing in a different kind of 'extreme' metal band. Like death metal '*rah-hhh*.' Or grimecore. Whatever-core, whatever they were. But I always wanted to play in a band that had melodic singing. And DragonForce were the first one I've been in that were a melodic band. But it started off with Sam and I, and we've been doing it ever since. I guess the secret is—it's fun. That's pretty much it. It's a fun thing, it's a fun band to play in and while it's fun we'll keep doing it. And when it's not fun anymore and we don't want to do it, we'll just stop!"

For guitars, Herman Li is a devoted Ibanez user, like so many metal musicians of the past thirty-five years. He said, "My main guitar is the Ibanez EGEN18. Some of the unique features of the guitar are the deeper cutaway on the lower horn, which enables extended access to the high frets. Also, the 21st to 24th frets are scalloped to give further control on the high notes. The guitar has a really fast neck so everything is so much easier to play on it, but at the same time it has very stable tuning and sustain with the help of Edge-Zero bridge. One more thing I love about this guitar is the diverse tones it can put out. The custom Di-Marzio HLM pickups can coil-split to create nine different combinations. The guitar can do full metal shred—all the way to ultra-clean tones for jazz."

> "WHAMMY BAR TECHNIQUES SEEMED TO BE A LOST ART FOR MANY YEARS. . . . BECAUSE I WAS REALLY INTO VIDEO GAMES AS A KID, I STARTED RELATING THEM TO THOSE SOUNDS AND GAVE THEM VIDEO-GAME NAMES."

told the author, "My early heroes were Richie Sambora, Marty Friedman, and Kirk Hammett. Later on, I got into players like Joe Satriani, Steve Vai, John Petrucci, and George Lynch. I think all the different guitar players I like influenced me in different ways, from

crazed harmonies with co-guitarist Sam Totman, tossing hot solos back and forth. It's pure virtuosity, proven by a YouTube video that's earned well over 100 million views.

Talking to Tiana Speter of thesoundcheck.org, Li remembers his pre-DragonForce days: "I was play-

HERMAN LI AND DRAGONFORCE AT THE 2015 DOWNLOAD FESTIVAL IN DONINGTON PARK, ENGLAND.

⚡ BRENT HINDS & BILL KELLIHER

Amid the technical virtuosity and polish of many 21st-century metal bands, Mastodon was a breath of refreshing doom. Instead of high-speed anthems, this Atlanta band revels in the churning grooves of Black Sabbath, Alice in Chains, and other purveyors of slow, moody riffage. Bill Kelliher and Brent Hinds avoid any hint of shredding, preferring to deliver massive tone and feel—and earning critical acclaim for it.

As Kelliher told FM99 WNOR Backstage Pass, "A lot of people make the assumption that, 'You're a metal band, you only listen to metal.' I barely listen to metal. When I was growing up, I listened to The Beatles, Led Zeppelin . . . Van Halen. Then I moved on to punk rock, and then . . . grunge. And then my metal bands were Iron Maiden, Slayer, Metallica, Voivod. When I want to put on something comfortable, that makes

the ESP LTD Sparrowhawk. Its shape is related to a non-reverse Firebird, with a maple-capped mahogany body and two Seymour Duncan Distortion humbuckers with push-pull coil taps (he also periodically grabs a single-cutaway ESP BK-600).

Regarding pickups, a choosy Kelliher told Ray McClelland of Guitarguitar.co.uk, "I have a lot of ESP Sparrowhawks. I have probably ten of them and a lot of them have different pickups in them, everything from the Lace Dissonant Aggressors to Lace Nitro Heavies, which sound great, to my new pickup which hasn't come out yet but I designed it with Mojotone. It's called the Hellbender. It's a very well-rounded sound, lots of bass response, just one of the best-sounding pickups so far. Also, Motor City pickups, I like those a lot; Bare Knuckle makes a great pickup. I used some Seymour Duncans, some

that tidal wave sound, emphasizing the groove over individual guitar heroics. Yet when Brent Hinds takes a solo, it's a high-velocity event that's in *no* way shred. It's pure, blistering metal.

For gear, Hinds is best known for his silverburst Gibson and Epiphone Flying V models. He's occasionally been known to rip on his beloved Gibson SGs and the retro-looking PRS Starla with a Bigsby vibrato.

Talking to Orange Amplifiers about his early gear, Hinds recalled, "Anything that sounded good you could get back in the day, we ended up playing. I was using like a Sovtek because that was the most affordable amp. Black Sabbath was the first band I ever saw using Orange amps when I was a kid, so I figure [they were] pretty good, I mean . . . *Sabbath*. That's like my favorite band. The first Sabbath albums are really inspiring because they're so dark and alluring. Also the tones are really classic . . . they sound really evil and awesome." ⚡

AMID THE TECHNICAL VIRTUOSITY . . . MASTODON IS A BREATH OF REFRESHING DOOM.

me feel like right at home, I'll put on an old Dead Kennedys record, or Soundgarden's *Louder Than Love*, or Bad Brains, or . . . Led Zeppelin."

For gear, rhythm guitarist Kelliher rocks a variety of signature Explorers from Gibson and the Electrical Guitar Company and a Gibson Les Paul Custom, though his most unique axe is

of those are in my Sparrowhawks, the distortion ones, they sound great."

On their 2014 set, *Once More 'Round the Sun*, Mastodon elegantly defined their wall-of-brute-force sound, with muscular guitarmanship over a bed of rhythm-section muscle. "The Motherload" is emblematic of

BILL KELLIHER AND BRENT HINDS OF MASTODON ESCHEW SHREDDING IN FAVOR OF MASSIVE TONE AND CHURNING RHYTHMS.

NITA STRAUSS & NILI BROSH

In the 1970s and '80s, Joan Jett, Lita Ford, and Jennifer Batten revolutionized the concept of women playing hard rock, but in the twenty-first century, Nita Strauss and Nili Brosh have redefined it as serious, respected shredders—once, a male-only category. Both musicians were co-guitarists in the Iron Maidens during the early 2010s, cranking out British metal and also setting the stage for their next career moves. Strauss vaulted from that tribute band to a full-time gig backing shock-rock icon Alice Cooper, while Brosh has worked with fellow shredder Tony MacAlpine, the cartoon band Dethklok, composer Danny Elfman, and Cirque du Soleil.

For influences, Strauss (born 1986) is a huge fan of Steve Vai and early shred pioneer Batten. Of her early days as a player, she told the web magazine *Rocksverige*, "I had a guitar which my dad had gotten me, but I didn't really play much. Then I saw the movie *Crossroads* with Steve Vai . . . I was like, 'Okay, that's what

Nita Strauss also made gear history, as she told Reverb, "In January of 2018, I became the first-ever female Ibanez signature artist. I am incredibly proud of the Ibanez JIVA, not just for what it represents . . . but we also designed a pretty freakin' cool guitar! It has a mahogany body, quilted maple top, and ebony fingerboard. It's super light and weighs six-and-a-half pounds. I play seven days a week—five shows with Alice Cooper and two clinics—[so] having a light guitar on your shoulder is amazing."

Hailing from Israel, Nili Brosh (born 1988) attended the Berklee College of Music in Boston and has worked with Guthrie Govan, Andy Timmons, Stu Hamm, and composer Danny Elfman. She's also released a number of solo albums. Brosh also plays Ibanez six- and now seven-string guitars. She said in an interview with Ibanez.com, "I usually play two guitars, including an RG927 quilted-maple top and Prestige 1527 maple. Up until a few years ago, I was a six-string play-

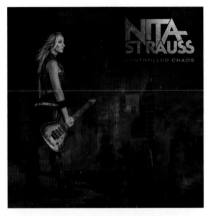

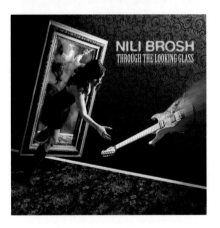

"I SHOOT FIRE OUT OF MY GUITAR!"

I'm supposed to be doing! I get it now.' Then I started listening to Guns N' Roses and stuff, but when I heard [Megadeth's] 'Trust', that's when I really got into heavy metal. I was listening to In Flames and Children of Bodom, Amon Amarth and At the Gates. I got really into the Scandinavian metal style, so that was one of my biggest and earliest influences."

er, so I had to pick up a seven-string for Tony MacAlpine's gig. I had to learn to use it very quickly and it was a little bit of a learning curve at first. Now it's pretty natural to me. When I have to play a lot of technically difficult phrases on this fast, thin neck, it's all very doable. I don't feel the guitar's working against me . . . it's helping me play the stuff I need to play."

In Nili Brosh's role with Cirque du Soleil, she was a costumed performer on stage, as opposed to sitting anonymously in a pit orchestra. She told Guitarguitar.co.uk, "I'm in this gold Jennifer Batten get-up onstage, basically running around with the other castmates. That was the whole point of that: to just be into the whole showmanship of the whole thing. . . . I still had to play difficult stuff, but you really can't buy that kind of live experience. Plus, I shot fire out of my guitar!"

LEFT: NITA STRAUSS VAULTED FROM AN IRON MAIDEN TRIBUTE BAND TO A FULL-TIME GIG WITH ALICE COOPER.
RIGHT: ISRAELI- BORN NILI BROSH PICKED UP THE SEVEN-STRING WHILE GIGGING WITH TONY MACALPINE.

METAL AFTER THE MILLENNIUM

TWENTY-FIRST-CENTURY TECH

In the new century, guitarists emerged at a fast and furious rate, as metal was showered with an endless parade of shred-leaning players. For arena-filling acts, Rammstein achieved global fame based on an inflammatory live show—in fact, they literally lit themselves on fire using flameproof suits and shot towering sprays of flames into the air. Mixing metal, electronica, dance beats, progressive, and dark dystopian moods (a sound dubbed Neue Deutsche Härte, translating to "new German hardness"), the group delivered stompers powered by guitarists Richard Kruspe and Paul Landers. Between their live show and powerhouse anthems like "Du Hast," Rammstein has evolved into one of the biggest metal bands in the world.

Among the technical virtuosos, Ron "Bumblefoot" Thal (born September 25, 1969) emerged in the 1990s as a shredder but landed a prime gig with Guns N' Roses in the 2000s, bringing his half-fretless Vigier doubleneck to "Sweet Child O' Mine" and other Guns N' Roses classics. Trivium featured dual flashes Matt Heafy and Corey Beaulieu, combining everything from thrash and groove metal to melodic power riffs. Greek axeman Gus G. (born September 12, 1980) nailed the coveted spot in Ozzy Osbourne's band and played on his 2010 *Scream* album. A monster technician, Gus could effortlessly play any of the timeless Rhoads/Lee/Wylde riffs and solos, as well as his own supersonic runs on a Jackson Gus G. Star solidbody. He currently plays in the Greek power-metal act Firewind.

Avenged Sevenfold has been a mega-act of the past twenty years, featuring lead guitarist Synyster Gates (born July 7, 1981), who plays a Schecter with upswept horns, his signature axe. As Gates told Schecter TV, "I needed [the guitar] to look ridiculous, and I needed 24 frets and a whammy bar. . . . I liked [the Avenger body] style, but knew I wanted [a different] headstock. We threw around some [design] ideas . . . I [don't remember] how the whole pinstripe idea came about, but it did, unfortunately. . . . We just released [a version] with the Sustainiac [pickup]. . . . Its primary use is as kind of an Ebow . . . but then you can do a lot of cool artificial harmonic and feedback emulations."

Diamond Rowe, a woman who plays alt-metal, made a splash via the group Tetrarch. Of her influences and gear, she told ESP, "There were many while I was learning guitar and growing up. Beyond James [Hetfield] and Kirk Hammett, there were other guys like Alexi [Laiho] from Children of Bodom, who is another favorite of mine. Him and Dan [Jacobs] from Atreyu, as well as Bill Kelliher of Mastodon. . . . I just got a brand new [ESP]. . . . It's the see-thru black EverTune EC-1000. . . . Also, it has Duncan [pickups]. It's crazy. All my other ESPs have EMGs. What I really like about them is that you can really hear the tone of the player. EMGs have their sound, and I like that too, but I feel like with the Duncans, you really hear the character of the player, which is new for me." ⚡

RESOURCES

Tony Iommi, interview with Pete Prown, *Guitar Shop* magazine, 1996

Ritchie Blackmore, interview with Pete Prown, *Vintage Guitar Magazine*, 2017

Martin Barre, interview with Pete Prown, *Guitar for the Practicing Musician* magazine, 1989

Mick Box, interview with Pete Prown, *Vintage Guitar Magazine*, 2018

Joe Walsh, interview with Ward Meeker, *Vintage Guitar Magazine*, 2012 https://www.vintageguitar.com/13423/joe-walsh/

Brian May, from page 62 of *Queen in Their Own Words*, book by Mick St. Michael, 1992

Robin Trower, interview with Martine Ehrenclou in *Rock and Blues Muse*, June 17, 2021 https://www.rockandbluesmusecom/2021/06/17/interview-robin-trower-guitar-legend/

Robin Trower, interview with Brian Holland in *Guitar International*, date unknown https://guitarinternational.com/2010/11/17/robin-trower-the-living-out-of-time-interview/

Joe Bouchard (Blue Öyster Cult), interview with Pete Prown, *Vintage Guitar Magazine*, 2016

Buck Dharma, interview with Willie Moseley of *Vintage Guitar Magazine*, 1998 https://www.vintageguitar.com/2830/buck-dharma

Rick Derringer, interview with Willie Mosely, *Vintage Guitar Magazine*, 2003

Rick Derringer, interview with Tom Guerra, date unknown https://tomguerra.com/tom-guerra-interviews-rick-derringer/

Joe Perry and Brad Whitford (Aerosmith), Jack Douglas interview with Ben Yakas of *The Gothamist*, July 21, 2016 https://gothamist.com/arts-entertainment/legendary-producer-jack-douglas-talks-aerosmith-bob-dylan-allen-ginsberg

Ronnie Montrose, interview with Pete Prown, *Guitar for the Practicing Musician* magazine, 1988

Frank Marino, web interview for *Hit-Channel.com*, 2012 https://www.hit-channel.com/frank-marino-mahogany-rushsolo/28143

Frank Marino, interview with Willie Mosley of *Vintage Guitar Magazine*, 2007 https://www.vintageguitar.com/3484/frank-marino-2/

Mick Ralphs, interview with Jamie Dickson, MusicRadar, 2013 https://www.musicradar.com/news/guitars/mick-ralphs-talks-mott-the-hoople-bowie-and-blouses-590250

Mick Ralphs, interview with Jamie Dickson, MusicRadar, 2013 https://www.musicradar.com/news/guitars/interview-mick-ralphs-of-mott-the-hoople-586056

Mick Ralphs, interview with *Vintage Guitar*, 2017 https://www.vintageguitar.com/31906/mick-ralphs-4/

Eddie Van Halen, interview with H. P. Newquist, *Guitar* magazine, 1998

Eddie Van Halen, interview with Pete Prown, *Guitar Shop* magazine, 1994

Ace Frehley, interview with Pete Prown, *Guitar for the Practicing Musician* magazine, 1990

Tom Scholz, interview with Ted Drozdowski for Gibson.com, 2008 http://www.thirdstage.ca/boston/articles/interviews/512-more-than-a-feeling-talking-les-pauls-with-bostons-tom-scholz

Nancy Wilson, interview with Johnny Zapp, *Vintage Guitar Magazine*, 2016

Neal Schon, interview with Ward Meeker in *Vintage Guitar Magazine*, 2021

Neal Schon, interview with Pete Prown, *Guitar Player* magazine, 1989

Angus Young, *Guitar* (Germany), 2021 https://bravewords.com/news/ac-dc-guitarist-angus-young-on-his-influences-when-i-look-at-all-the-players-who-i-admire-you-can-go-from-a-to-z-video

Pat Travers, interview with Gary James at ClassicBands.com, date unknown http://classicbands.com/PatTraversInterview.html

Pat Travers, interview with Pete Prown, *Guitar* magazine, 1993

Ritchie Blackmore, interview with H. P. Newquist, date unknown

Michael Schenker, interview with Pete Prown, 2013

Scott Gorham and Brian Robertson, interviews with Pete Prown

Glenn Tipton, website https://glenntipton.com/guitar-collection.asp

Uli Roth, interview with Andy Craven for Dinosaur Rock Guitar, 2008 http://www.dinosaurrockguitar.com/node/233

Adrian Smith, interview with Pete Prown, *Vintage Guitar Magazine*, 2020

Dave Murray, interview with Bret Adams, *Vintage Guitar Magazine*, 2021 https://www.vintageguitar.com/39763/dave-murray/

Randy Rhoads, Pete Prown interview with Kelly Garni, 1990s

Randy Rhoads, interview with Pete Prown, *Vintage Guitar Magazine*, 2011 https://www.vintageguitar.com/9495/randy-rhoads/

Randy Rhoads, Steve Vai quote from the documentary film *Ozzy Osbourne: Thirty Years after the Blizzard*

Rich Williams, interview with Bret Adams, *Vintage Guitar Magazine*, 2018 https://www.vintageguitar.com/35009/rich-ard-williams/

Kerry Livgren, interview with Brian D. Holland of *Guitar International*, 2010 https://guitarinternational.com/2010/12/24/kerry-livgren-talks-kansas-guitars-and-proto-kaw/

Alex Lifeson, interview with Pete Prown, 1993

Michael Wilton and Chris DeGarmo (Queensrÿche), interview with Pete Prown, *Guitar Shop* magazine, 1995

John Petrucci, interview with Tom Quayle, *Guitar Interactive Magazine*, 2017 https://www.guitarinteractivemagazine.com/features/feature-john-petrucci-interviewing-your-heroes/

John Petrucci on his Ernie Ball guitar, Ernie Ball press video https://www.youtube.com/watch?v=dJu1ih-B2YCM

Phil Collen, interview with Nick Bowcott of Sweetwater, 2021 https://www.sweetwater.com/insync/def-leppards-phil-collen-talks-hysteria-songwriting-and-more/

Gary Moore, interview with Pete Prown (as Gary Green), *Guitar Player* magazine, 1990

Joan Jett, interview with Nick Cracknell, MusicRadar, 2008 https://www.musicradar.com/totalguitar/joan-jett-launches-signature-axe-248002

Lita Ford, interview with Paul Rigg, Guitars Exchange, date unknown https://guitarsexchange.com/en/unplugged/284/lita-ford-interview/

Brad Gillis, interview with Willie Mosely, *Vintage Guitar Magazine*, 2001
https://www.vintageguitar.com/2907/brad-gillis/

Mick Mars, interview with Joe Bosso, MusicRadar, 2008
https://www.musicradar.com/news/guitars/musicradar-interview-motley-crues-mick-mars-165974

John Sykes, interview with Mick Burgett, Metal Express Radio, 2008
https://www.metalexpressradiocom/2008/01/28/interview-with-john-sykes-thin-lizzy/

John Sykes, interview with Steve Newton of earofnewt.com, 2014
https://earofnewt.com/2014/06/15/ex-thin-lizzy-guitarist-john-sykes-on-blue-murder-bob-rock-and-the-little-mountain-sound/

Vernon Reid, interview with S. H. Fernando Jr. of Red Bull Music Academy, 2014
https://daily.redbullmusicacademy.com/2014/12/vernon-reid-interview

Vernon Reid, interview with ESP Guitars, 2017
https://www.espguitars.com/articles/2004996-vernon-reid-on-the-ltd-cult-86

Steve Vai, interview with Jonathan Graham, *Guitar Interactive Magazine*, 2020
https://www.guitarinteractivemagazine.com/features/steve-vai-interview/

Steve Vai, interview with Stuff.co.nz, 2012
https://www.stuff.co.nz/entertainment/6577334/The-Steve-Vai-Interview

Steve Vai, interview with Pete Prown, 2021

Joe Satriani, interviews with Pete Prown, *Guitar Shop* magazine (1995) and *Vintage Guitar Magazine* (2008)
https://www.vintageguitar.com/3571/joe-satriani-2/

Joe Satriani, from *Ibanez: The Untold Story*, by Paul Specht, 2005

Vivian Campbell, interview with Willie Mosely, *Vintage Guitar Magazine*, 2006
https://www.vintageguitar.com/2999/vivian-campbell/

Vivian Campbell, interview with Robert Cavuoto, My Global Mind, 2016
https://myglobalmind.com/2016/02/14/interview-with-vivian-campbell-guitars-last-in-line-def-leppard-former-dio/

Paul Gilbert, interview with Ruben Mosqueda of Sleaze Roxx, 2021
https://sleazeroxx.com/interviews/interview-with-mr-big-guitarist-solo-artist-paul-gilbert/

George Lynch, from *Legends of Rock Guitar*, book by Pete Prown and H. P. Newquist, 1997

George Lynch, interview with David Szabados of Legendary Tones, 2004
https://legendarytones.com/george-lynch-interview/

George Lynch, interview with Tony Bacon for Reverb, 2020
https://reverb.com/news/kirk-hammett-george-lynch-and-esps-emergence

Tony MacAlpine, interview with Thom Jennings of Backstageaxxess.com, 2011
https://backstageaxxess.com/2011/08/tony-macalpine-interview/

Vinnie Moore, interview with Pete Prown

James Hetfield, interview with James Perlah, *Newsweek*, February 9, 2017
https://www.newsweek.com/metallicas-james-hetfield-rides-lightning-newsweek-553333

Kirk Hammett, Gibson TV *Icons* show, 2020
https://www.youtube.com/watch?v=bPy8Y-yUgxyA

Dave Mustaine, interview with Spencer Kaufman of Consequence of Sound/Heavy Consequence, 2020
https://megadeth.com/news/2020/dave-mustaine-talks-rust-in-peace-dimebag-and-new-megadeth-album/

Jeff Hanneman (Slayer), ESP Guitars, 2009
https://www.espguitars.com/videos/2042304

Kerry King, interview with Tommy Colletti, The Music Zoo, 2011
https://www.themusiczoo.com/blogs/news/exclusive-interview-kerry-king-of-slayer

Scott Ian, interview with Stereogum, 2022
https://www.stereogum.com/2185693/scott-ian-anthrax-motor-sister-vh1-public-enemy-meat-loaf/interviews/weve-got-a-file-on-you/

Scott Ian, interview with David Slavković of Ultimate-Guitar.com, 2020
https://www.ultimate-guitar.com/news/interviews/anthrax_scott_ian_explains_why_he_stuck_with_jackson_guitars_for_so_long_talks_randy_rhoads_connection.html

Slash, interview with Matt Allen in *Kerrang!* magazine, 2021
https://www.kerrang.com/slash-guns-n-roses-were-a-gang-that-walked-into-a-room-like-you-dont-want-to-f-ck-with-us

Slash, interview with Nick Bowcott of Sweetwater, 2020
https://youtu.be/790DFXbC7CQ

Zakk Wylde, interview with Nick Bowcott of Sweetwater, 2018
https://www.youtube.com/watch?v=wR-J36ERAD98

Zakk Wylde, interviews with Pete Prown, *Vintage Guitar Magazine*, 1995, 2019

Dimebag Darrell, interviews with Pete Prown, *Guitar for the Practicing Musician* magazine (1991) and *Vintage Guitar Magazine* (2020)

Ty Tabor, interview with Pete Prown, *Guitar for the Practicing Musician*, December 1991

Munky (Korn), from *Ibanez: The Untold Story*, by Paul Specht, 2005

Jeff Loomis, interview with Justin Beck of Ultimate-Guitar.com, 2017
https://www.ultimate-guitar.com/news/interviews/jeff_loomis_what_made_me_want_to_play_7-string_guitar.html

Jerry Cantrell, interview with Sean Allen of IGN, 2013
https://www.youtube.com/watch?v=Ip-G4yDBnjfo&t=188s

Jerry Cantrell, interview with Nick Bowcott of Sweetwater, "Guitar Rig Tour" video, 2018
https://www.youtube.com/watch?v=1W-WSPb1qh-I

Tom Morello, Red Bull TV *Gearheads* show, 2016
https://reverb.com/news/tom-morello-thinks-gear-doesnt-matter

Tom Morello, interview with *Concertlivewire.com*, 2008
http://www.concertlivewire.com/morelloint.htm

Pearl Jam gear, interview with Peter Seidel, *Guitar Shop* magazine, 1994

Kim Thayil, interview with Wolf Marshall, *Vintage Guitar Magazine*, 2021
https://www.vintageguitar.com/37755/fretprints-kim-thayil/

Kim Thayil, interview with Rich Maloof, *Guitar* magazine, 1996
http://web.stargate.net/soundgarden/articles/guitar_7-96.shtml

Adam Jones (Tool), interview with Dutch television show *Onrust!*, 1994
https://www.youtube.com/watch?v=f7A1cM-fl0Xc

Mike Scaccia (Ministry), statement by Philip Anselmo, 2012
https://metalinsider.net/in-memoriam/philip-anselmo-and-dave-brockie-oderus-urungus-comment-on-mike-scaccias-passing

Page Hamilton (Helmet), interview with Baker Rorick, *Guitar Shop* magazine, 1994

John Christ (Danzig), interview with Pete Prown, *Guitar Shop* magazine, 1995

Jay Yuenger, interview with Machinemusic.net ("Still Zombie after All These Years"), 2015
https://machinemusic.net/2015/08/04/still-zombie-after-all-these-years-an-interview-with-jay-yuenger/

Chuck Schuldiner, interview with Mark Morton at Examiner.com, 1995
https://braveworlds.com/news/death-exclusive-uncirculated-inteview-with-chuck-schuldiner-from-1995-released-online

Bill Steer (Carcass), Listen to Heavy Metal blog, 2010
https://listentoheavymetal.wordpress.com/2010/12/04/interview-bill-steer-carcass/

Trey Azagthoth (Morbid Angel), interview with Disposable Underground, 1991
https://disposableunderground.com/morbid-angel-interview-with-trey-azagthoth-from-the-vault/

Mikael Åkerfeldt (Opeth), interview with Metal Injection, 2014
https://metalinjection.net/video/opeth-interview-2014-new-album-satanism-and-whats-heavy

John 5, interview with Catherine Ash of Reverb, 2016
https://reverb.com/news/reverb-interview-john-5

Mårten Hagström (Meshuggah), interview with Rauta, 2018
https://www.youtube.com/watch?v=UKI_pqBZFkM&t=2s

Joel Stroetzel (Killswitch Engage), interview with Ivan Chopik of Guitar Messenger, 2009
https://guitarmessenger.com/joel-stroetzel-interview-killswitch-engage/

Ben Weinman (Dillinger Escape Plan), interview with Jon Robertson of Bearded Gentleman Music, 2013
https://beardedgentlemenmusic.com/2013/07/02/interview-with-dillinger-escape-plans-ben-weinman/

Mark Tremonti, interview with Ward Meeker, Vintage Guitar Magazine, 2012
https://www.vintageguitar.com/13821/mark-tremonti/

Mark Tremonti, interview with Anne Erickson of Reverb, 2014
https://reverb.com/news/reverb-interview-mark-tremonti

Alexi Laiho, quote from Dimmu Borgir guitarist on Loudersound.com, 2021
https://www.loudersound.com/features/alexi-laiho-children-of-bodom-life-story

Alexi Laiho, interview with Mark Cowles, Performer magazine, 2014
https://performermag.com/new-music-and-video/interviews-and-features/exclusive-interview-with-alexi-laiho-from-children-of-bodom/

Alexi Laiho, interview with Total Guitar, 2013
https://www.youtube.com/watch?v=hx-kUL-X093c

Herman Li (DragonForce), interview with Pete Prown, Vintage Guitar Magazine

Herman Li, interview with The Soundcheck, 2017 https://www.thesoundcheck.org/post/lightning-round-interview-herman-li-dragonforce

Bill Kelliher (Mastodon), interview with Elif Ozden for FM99 WNOR Backstage Pass, 2021
https://metalheadzone.com/bill-kelliher-addresses-mastodons-influences-i-barely-listen-to-metal/

Bill Kelliher, interview with Ray McClelland of GuitarGuitar.co.uk (a British retail store), 2021 https://www.guitarguitar.co.uk/news/141472/

Brent Hinds, interview with Orange Amplifiers, 2018
https://www.youtube.com/watch?v=Cr3xB-vCl1no

Nita Strauss, interview with Niclas Müller-Hansen of Rocksverige (Swedish web magazine), 2018
https://www.rocksverige.se/intervju-nita-strauss-fran-alice-cooper/

Nita Strauss, interview with Reverb, 2018
https://reverb.com/news/video-nita-strauss-on-her-ibanez-jiva10-signature-teaches-pandemonium-chorus-riff

Nili Brosh, interview with Ibanez.com, 2012
https://www.youtube.com/watch?v=IHyDX-GiaFj4

Nili Brosh, interview with guitarguitar.co.uk, 2021
https://www.guitarguitar.co.uk/news/141436/

Synyster Gates (Avenged Sevenfold), interview with Schecter TV, 2013
https://www.youtube.com/watch?v=hL9NyPenlXA

Diamond Rowe (Tetrach), interview with ESP Guitars, 2017
https://www.espguitars.com/articles/2008488-artist-spotlight-diamond-rowe-tetrach

IMAGE CREDITS

B = bottom, L = left, R = right, T = top
Alamy Stock Photos: 2-3, ZUMA press; 11, Pictorial Press; 13, Pictorial Press; 17, Mirrorpix; 23, Pictorial Press; 25, Yui Mok; 27, marka/press holland; 33, Odile Noël; 37, Gijsbert Hanekroot; 39, Pictorial Press; 43, Pictorial Press; 45, MHP; 55, Pictorial Press; 59, Media Punch; 61, Archive PL; 67, Terje Dokken; 69T, Media Punch; 69B, ZUMA Press; 71, Goddard Archive; 77, Pictorial Press; 81T&B, Media Punch; 87, John Atashian; 91T&B, Philip Buonpastore; 93, ZUMA Press; 95, Media Punch; 97, ZUMA Press; 103, Odile Noël/Lebrecht Music & Arts; 105R, dpa; 109, Media Punch; 111, Pictorial Press; 113, John Atashian; 117, ZUMA Press; 121, Pictorial Press; 123, steve orobec; 125, Media Punch; 127, ZUMA Press; 129, John Atashian; 131T, ZUMA Press; 131B, WENN; 133T, Media Punch; 133BL, ZUMA Press; 133BR, Katja Ogrin; 137T, Pacific Press; 137B, WENN; 139, Michael Bush; 143, Katja Ogrin; 145, ZUMA Press; 149, Media Punch; 151, WENN; 153, Pictorial Press; 157, John Atashian; 159, ZUMA Press; 161, WENN; 163T, 3SongsNo-Flash; 163BL, Zuma Press; 166, Christian Hjorth; 167, Sam Kovak; 169, Nikolaj Bransolm; 170, Terje Dokken; 171, ZUMA Press; 175, E.M.; 177, Katja Ogrin; 179, Katja Ogrin; 181L, ZUMA Press; 181R, Born Cavrag; 183L, dpa; 183R, Glenn Francis; 185TL, Ricky Bassman; 185TR, floreny Boyadjian; 185BL, Katja Ogrin. **Getty Images**: 15, David Redfern/Redferns; 19L, Michael Ochs Archives; 29, Larry Hulst/Michael Ochs Archives; 31, Rob Verhorst/Redferns; 41, Koh Hasebe/Shinko Music; 47, Jorgen Angel/Redferns; 49, Michael Putland/Hulton Archive; 51, Larry Hulst/Michael Ochs Archives; 53, Michael Putland/Hulton Archive; 63, Richard E. Aaron/Redferns; 65, Chris Walter/WireImage; 75, Michael Putland/Hulton Archive; 79, Erica Echenberg/Redferns; 83T, Marc S. Canter/Michael Ochs Archives; 83B, Paul Natkin; 85, Jeffrey Mayer/WireImage; 101, Duncan Raban, Popperfoto; 105L, Terry Lott/Sony Music Archive; 107, Paul Natkin; 119, C Brandon/Redferns; 141, Anne Summa/Hulton Archive; 155, Ebet Roberts/Redferns; 163BR, Bob Berg; 168, Brigitte Engl/Redferns. **Seth Steffenhagen Photography**: 185BR **Unsplash**: endpapers, Ankit G.

ACKNOWLEDGMENTS

Thanks to editor Dennis Pernu for his wise and steady hand during this project. Also deep appreciation to Ward Meeker, the talented writers, and staff of Vintage Guitar Magazine; H. P. Newquist for historical guitar perspective and interviews; Rich Maloof; the talented members of my most excellent band Quattro Formaggi; and, of course, my wife, children, sons- and daughters-in-law, and growing number of grandchildren—all of whom are surely future metalheads.

INDEX

Quarto.com
© 2023 Quarto Publishing Group USA Inc.
Text © 2023 Pete Prown

First Published in 2023 by Motorbooks, an imprint of The Quarto Group,
100 Cummings Center, Suite 265-D, Beverly, MA 01915, USA.
T (978) 282-9590 F (978) 283-2742

Motorbooks titles are also available at discount for retail, wholesale, promotional, and bulk
purchase. For details, contact the Special Sales Manager by email at specialsales@quarto.
com or by mail at The Quarto Group, Attn: Special Sales Manager, 100 Cummings Center,
Suite 265-D, Beverly, MA 01915, USA.

27 26 25 24 23   1 2 3 4 5

ISBN: 978-0-7603-7775-8

Digital edition published in 2023
eISBN: 978-0-7603-7776-5

Names: Prown, Pete, author.
Title: Ultimate heavy metal guitars : from hard rock to metal / Pete Prown.

Description: Beverly, MA : Motorbooks, 2023. | Includes index. | Summary:
   "Expansive history profiles dozens of heavy metal guitarists from the
   1970s to today, featuring performance photography and an authoritative
   text detailing the careers and gear of each"-- Provided by publisher.
Identifiers: LCCN 2022061448 | ISBN 9780760377758 | ISBN 9780760377765
   (ebook)
Subjects: LCSH: Rock musicians. | Electric guitar. | Guitar--Electronic
   equipment. | Rock music--History and criticism. | Heavy metal
   (Music)--History and criticism.
Classification: LCC ML1015.G9 P78 2023 | DDC 787.87/19--dc23/eng/20221223
LC record available at https://lccn.loc.gov/2022061448

Design: Justin Page
Cover Image: Justin Page
Page Layout: Justin Page

Printed in China